Great Americana

Indian Captivity

Oliver M. Spencer

almost froze my blood, raise his rifle to his shoulder, intending to shoot me." Fortunately the other Indian persuaded his companion not to shoot and Spencer escaped with a brutal beating. In the Indian village, he was placed in the custody of a squaw for whom he performed various domestic tasks. In spite of the harsh treatment he often received from her, a bond of mutual affection developed between the boy and the squaw. On one occasion she recounted to Spencer the injustices the Indians had suffered from the "palefaces." She lamented "their rapid growth, their widely-spreading population, their increasing strength and power, their insatiable avarice, and their continued encroachments on the red men," and she predicted "that they would not be satisfied until they had crowded the Indians to the extreme north, to perish on the great Ice lake; or to the far west" where those who escaped the white men's rifles would be pushed into the sea. "All would at length be exterminated."

Word eventually got back that Spencer was an Indian prisoner and arrangements for his release were effected through the British in Canada. After having spent seven months in captivity, he was brought to Detroit and from there made his way to some of his family in New Jersey. Not until 1795 did he find an opportunity to undertake the long trip back to Ohio to rejoin his parents.

Milo M. Quaife gives additional background about Spencer in his edition of *The Indian Captivity of O. M. Spencer* (Chicago, 1917), pp. ix-xxv. To compare Spencer's narrative of captivity among the Indians with others of the same period see Ralph L. Rusk, *The Literature of the Middle Western Frontier* (New York, 1962), I, 89-95.

SUNDAY SCHOOL

YOUTH's LIBRARY

Temple of Truth.

PUBLISHED FOR THE

METHODIST EPISCOPAL CHURCH.

SPENCER'S REMOVAL TO OHIO

See Page 5.

INDIAN CAPTIVITY:

A TRUE NARRATIVE

OF THE

CAPTURE OF THE REV. O. M. SPENCER

BY THE INDIANS,

IN THE NEIGHBOURHOOD OF CINCINNATI.

WRITTEN BY HIMSELF.

NEW-YORK,

PUBLISHED BY B. WAUGH AND T. MASON,

For the Sunday School Union of the Methodist Episcopal Church,
at the Conference Office, 200 Mulberry-street.

J. Collord, Printer.

1835.

Indian Captivity

by Oliver M. Spencer

READEX MICROPRINT

Foreword

Indian Captivity: A True Narrative of the Capture of the Rev. O. M. Spencer was published in book form in 1835 after having previously appeared in the *Western Christian Advocate* and in the *Christian Advocate and Journal*. In it Spencer describes his capture by the Indians in Ohio when he was a boy some forty years before. Aside from being a good adventure story, Spencer's account illustrates the uncertainties of life on the frontier and provides an excellent picture of the Indians who were reluctantly falling back before the tide of settlers moving West. Spencer's many reflections about the West as he had known it as a boy compared to "now," indicate how rapidly the country had changed in forty years.

Spencer's father had served as a colonel in the Revolutionary Army but emerged from the war in straitened circumstances. Unable to improve his fortune in New Jersey, he determined to try his luck in the West. Though Spencer's mother was strongly attached to family and friends in New Jersey, she accepted her husband's decision without a word of complaint. The family set out for Ohio in 1790, making the trip over the mountains under the most difficult conditions. "Those who now travel from Philadelphia to Pittsburg, ascending easily and gliding rapidly over the Alleghany, along the broad and finely-paved road; finding, at convenient distances, commodious inns and excellent entertainment, can form but a faint idea of the difficulties and dangers encountered, and the fatigue and privations, which more than 'forty years since' were endured by emigrants to the west," Spencer said.

Spencer's family settled in the vicinity of Cincinnati. Stories of Indian atrocities committed against other settlers kept them in a state of alarm all the time. In July, 1792, young Spencer and several others were traveling by boat on the Ohio when they were surprised by two Indians. Spencer was taken prisoner. As he was being marched away, he attempted to escape, but the Indians soon found him again. "Methinks I can now see the horrible savage grinding his teeth with rage, and with a look of fiendish malice, that

INTRODUCTION.

———

THE following narrative was written for the Western Christian Advocate, and copied from that paper into the Christian Advocate and Journal, and is at this time in a course of publication in some other papers in the country.— These publications of Mr. Spencer's narrative show in what light it is viewed by the public, and that it has been read by thousands with interest. Believing that it would produce a still wider and more lasting interest in the form of a book, the agents of the Methodist Book Concern have obtained the consent of Mr. Spencer to publish and sell it in that form for the benefit of the connection, and with a view especially to the improvement of our youth and children. They have been at the expense of procuring a number of cuts for the work, and have spared no expense to make it both interesting and profitable to the reader.

December, 1834.

INDIAN CAPTIVITY.

CHAPTER I.

In October, 1790, young Spencer removes with his father's family from New Jersey to Columbia, in the state of Ohio—Badness of the roads—A gloomy night on the Alleghany—Descend the Ohio River—Arrive safely at Columbia.

It was on a pleasant day in October, of the year 1790, when only nine years of age, I mounted the leading horse attached to the foremost of two wagons destined to the " far west," in which my mother and sisters were seated ; and in which were stowed such articles of household furniture as were indispensable to the comfort of a family, and which could not then be easily procured west of the Alleghany. With spirits naturally buoyant—pleased with the novelty of travelling, from which I anticipated a great deal of pleasure, the few tears which I shed on quitting for ever the home of my childhood, were soon dried up ; and I wondered not a little at the sober sadness of my father, the deep sighs of my mother, and the frequent sobs of my sisters, whose feelings and expectations I supposed would naturally correspond with mine.

My father had descended from one of the first families who left England on account of the persecutions for religious opinions, in the reign of the second Charles, to seek in the unbroken wilds of New-England an asylum from oppression, and to rear a temple to the God of their fathers, in which they might worship him " according to the dictates of their own consciences."

Inheriting the spirit of his ancestors, he was among the first to resist the pretensions of Great Britain, and to arm in defence of our rights and liberties. Having signalized himself on several occasions, particularly in the battle of Spring-field, N. J., at the head of a battalion of militia, he was appointed by congress to the command of a regiment, which he led in the battles of Brandywine, Germantown, and Monmouth ; and at the head of which he continued until the close of the war.

Before entering the continental army, he possessed a small fortune, the fruits of his industry in a lucrative business ; but of this, a large amount was destroyed by the enemy, and more than ten thousand dollars, advanced by him in specie to pay and clothe his regiment, were *repaid to him by congress, in continental money,* on which he sustained a total loss. Like many of his companions in arms, after encountering the dangers and enduring the hardships of a protracted war, Col. Spencer found himself at its close reduced from affluence to comparative poverty ; but with them too he enjoyed the proud satisfaction of having aided in achieving that independence which laid the foundation of our national greatness and prosperity, and the hope of perpetuating to his children's children the blessings of civil and religious liberty.

With impaired health, and injured constitution, he again engaged in business, hoping in time to retrieve his losses, and trusting in the honour and justice of the government to pay his equitable claims against it; but in this hope, and in this confidence, he was deeply disappointed.— After toiling many years with little success, hearing the flattering accounts then in circulation of the beauty and fertility of the Miami country, he determined to explore it. He *did* visit it in 1789, and being much pleased with it, determined on making it his future residence. Previously to his leaving home, he had disposed of his certificates for his military services at one third part of their nominal value, and vested their proceeds in Miami lands; and now, having purchased some lots, and erected a cabin in Columbia for the reception of his family, he returned home to effect their removal. Neither my father's description of the Miami country, nor the most glowing representations almost daily published, of "*the land flowing with milk and honey,*" could have prevailed with my mother to abandon the home of her fathers, "her own, her native land;" the early companions of her youth; her faithful and long-tried friends; and above all, some of her own daughters, who had married and settled around her: but she was a most exemplary wife, sensible and intelligent, possessing great resolution and uncommon fortitude, and, withal, a woman of deep piety; and being satisfied that the step on which my father had de-

cided was necessary, she acquiesced in that decision without murmuring.

The first few days of our journey passed very
heavily. There was indeed much that amused,
and even delighted me; but we had little conversation; my thoughtless whistle, and the quaint
expressions and occasional humorous sayings of
the driver, an old soldier, being all that for hours
broke upon the stillness of the lonely woods, or
varied the dull monotony of our rumbling wheels.
Gradually, however, the family became more
cheerful. Dwelling less upon the past, their
thoughts began to be occupied with their present
condition and future prospects, and they now
found much to interest them and to render their
journey agreeable.

From Mendham, a small village in East Jersey, (our late residence,) our route lay through
Easton and Harrisburg. Passing these towns,
we soon reached the formidable mountains which
separate the waters of the Atlantic states from
those of the Mississippi valley; and here we
were called to exert all our fortitude, and to exercise all our patience. Those who now travel
from Philadelphia to Pittsburg, ascending easily
and gliding rapidly over the Alleghany, along
the broad and finely-paved road; finding, at
convenient distances, commodious inns and excellent entertainment, can form but a faint idea
of the difficulties and dangers encountered, and
the fatigue and privations, which more than
" forty years since" were endured by emigrants
to the west, from extremely bad roads, and worse

accommodations. Often since, when travelling the road from Chambersburg to Pittsburg, in a comfortable stage, at a rapid rate, over the precipitous Laurel hill and formidable Alleghany, I have been forcibly struck with the contrast ; and as I occasionally caught a glimpse of the ancient narrow road winding among the trees, now rising, now descending abruptly by steep steps of solid rock, I thought it scarcely possible that any vehicle had ever passed over it : it was travelled, certainly, at the risk of limbs and even of life.

It was after a day's fatiguing journey over the worst portion of this road, in which we were delayed more than an hour in repairing damages of one of our wagons from a disastrous overset, that night overtook us in the midst of a dense forest, more than two miles from any habitation. This to our family, who had never known the want of a comfortable shelter, was a novel, and indeed an almost appalling circumstance. To increase their apprehension, the wolves commenced a most hideous howling, and their fruitful imaginations soon added a host of bears, and panthers, and robbers. Presently, however, with the aid of a tinder box, we kindled a large fire ; and after a slender repast of biscuit and cheese, with a little pure water from an adjoining brook, we retired to our wagons, and in deep sleep soon forgot our cares and apprehensions. We had slept, perhaps, two hours, when awaking about eleven o'clock, I discovered that my bed fellow, (a nephew a year my elder,) had left the wagon. After waiting some time, as he did not return, I called him, and repeating my calls louder and still louder, soon awoke the family. Search was made for him in every probable direction, but in vain ; loud calls and the firing of guns received no response, save the louder howling of the wolves, whom we now confidently believed had torn him to pieces. But in the midst of our alarm and distress we received the welcome information of his safety. He had walked in his sleep, with bare feet and almost naked, in a cold night of October, to a house about two miles in advance of us on our road, had knocked at the door, and was admitted, but did not awake until the screams of its inmates, some of whom were terror stricken, aroused him. Recovering himself, he soon convinced them that he was not an apparition, but a real "spirit of health," and as it was now late, was kindly accommodated with a bed for the night. It is a fact within the recollection of many of us, that not more than twenty-five years since, before the application of steam to the propulsion of vessels, almost the only conveyance on the western waters was by keel and flat boats. The latter, being cheap, and easily built, and intended wholly for conveyance down the Ohio and Mississippi, were always sought by families descending these rivers. And as there were several places along the Monongahela at which these boats were built, and where they could be obtained on better terms than at Pittsburg, instead of taking the direct road to that place, we took a south-westerly direction to Jacob's creek, a branch of the

Yougheghany. Here, having arrived and waited more than a month for the building of a boat, and for a rise of water, we embarked for Columbia; and in company with another family, and numbering together about sixteen souls, soon found ourselves quietly gliding down the beautiful waters of the Ohio.

To the early emigrant it must be truly pleasing to mark the great and rapid changes which within his remembrance have been wrought, not only along the rivers, but in the whole valley of the Mississippi. To contrast the once unbroken wilderness, in its solitude undisturbed, save by the howl of the wolf, the terrific scream of the panther, or the appalling yell of the savage, with the cultivated fields and comfortable farm houses, the neat villages, the populous towns, and even large cities which he now beholds, risen as by magic, and swarming with inhabitants, active, industrious, and enterprising; to hear the "busy hum," and note the constant bustle of commerce; and where the sluggish flat, or labouring keel seemed scarcely to advance, to see the stately steamer proudly stemming the rapid current, or urged down it at so swift a speed, as seemingly to bring near places the most remote, and to overcome, in the short time of eight days, a distance, to perform which once required three months, even in the best keel boat, with all the aid of sails, and oars, and warps.

Yet there are times when he enjoys a melancholy pleasure in his recollections of the past; when the varied scenery of the west was beheld by him in all its loveliness, and in all its primeval grandeur. When unused to the destructive wave of the steamer, or the more desolating axe of the later settler, the unbroken banks of the beautiful Ohio were seen, on one side, first gently sloping from the pebbled shore fringed with willows, then gradually ascending a few rods, covered with cotton wood, linden, and soft maple, then with steep ascent rising to their summit, crowned with elm and sycamore, and bounding the ample bottom, where the stately beech and poplar, the noble ash and walnut, the tall hickory, and the majestic oak, had withstood the storms of ages. Here too were seen the flowering buckeye, the guarded honey tree, dropping its sweets, the fragrant spicewood and sassafras, affording tea, and the maple, yielding sugar to the early settlers. On the other side were seen the hills bounding these fertile bottoms, and forming a vast amphitheatre ; sometimes breaking abruptly in huge masses of rock, interspersed with cedar, and opposing an unyielding barrier to the stream ; and now terminating with precipitous descent, covered with lofty trees quite down to the water's edge. There seemed to be blended with the beauty, and the lovely scenery of the Ohio, inspiring pleasure, a wildness and a solitude, which struck the beholder with mingled fear and awe.

Such were our sensations as we descended the Ohio. Indeed, there was with us a prevailing sense of loneliness ; a feeling of apprehension, which after we left Pittsburg was interrupted only as we passed by Wheeling, Marietta, Kanawha, Galliopolis, Limestone, (now Maysville,) and a few other intermediate settlements, to our place of destination. But although we were sometimes alarmed, and often apprehended an attack from the Indians, we saw none, nor but few signs of any, during our passage; and providentially meeting with no disaster, arrived safely at Columbia, early in December, 1790.

———

CHAPTER II.

Ancient site of Columbia—Description of Spencer's first house—Alarming news of an attack by the Indians on Dunlap's Station—Hazardous enterprise of Mr. John S. Wallace—Volunteers march to relieve the garrison—Burning of Mr. A. Hunt by the Indians, and the shock it produced—Depredations by the Indians—General St. Clair is sent by government to subdue the Indians—His defeat.

IT is, perhaps, unknown to many, that the broad and extensive plain stretching along the Ohio from the Crawfish to the mouth, and for three miles up the Little Miami, and now divided into farms, highly cultivated, was the ancient site of Columbia, a town laid out by Major Benjamin Stites, its original proprietor; and by him and others once expected to become a large city, the great capital of the west. From Crawfish, the small creek forming its northwestern boundary, more than one mile up the Ohio, and extending back about three fourths of a mile, and half way up the high hill which formed a part of its eastern and northern limits, the ground was laid off into blocks, containing each eight lots of half an acre, bounded by streets intersecting at right angles. The residue of the plain was divided into lots of four and five acres, for the accommodation of the town. Over this plain, on our arrival, we found scattered about fifty cabins, flanked by a small stockade nearly half a mile below the mouth of the Miami, together with a few block houses for the protection of the inhabitants, at suitable distances along the bank of the Ohio. Whoever has travelled the turnpike road leading from Cincinnati to Milford, after crossing the large culvert over Crawfish, and passing the cluster of buildings beyond it, has seen, a few hundred yards farther on, near the foot of the hill on the left of that road, an old hewed log house, with four small windows in front, until within a few years past shaded with large willows. About six feet north of that house, built forty-two years since, and long the residence of my father, stood the small log cabin, our first humble shelter on our landing. Its narrow doors of thick oak plank, turning on stout wooden hinges, and secured with strong bars braced with timber from the floor, formed a safe barrier to the entrance below; while above, on every side were port holes, or small embrasures, from which we might see, and fire upon the enemy. Of windows we had but two, containing only four panes of glass each, in openings so small, that any attempt to enter them by force must have proved fatal to an assailant.

We had occupied our new habitation about a month, adding greatly to its accommodation, and supplying many conveniences around us; indeed, we began to submit to the inconveniences, privations, hardships, and dangers common to the pioneers of the west, without much repining; and having heard of no disturbances by Indians, in our immediate neighbourhood, for some time previously, felt little apprehension of danger.— But our fears were suddenly aroused by the news of an attack made by several hundred Indians on Dunlap's station, (now Colerain,) fifteen or twenty miles northwest of Cincinnati, then garrisoned by a few inhabitants, and thirty or forty soldiers, under the command of Lieut. Kingsbury. This intelligence was brought by Mr. John S. Wallace, (now Colonel Wallace, our respected fellow citizen,) who at the risk of his life left the garrison at night, passed unperceived through the enemy, and safely reached Cincinnati the same night. Of the volunteers, who marched immediately to relieve the garrison, one company was from Columbia. All were well mounted, and armed with rifles, knives, and some even with tomahawks, and dressed in hunting shirts, moved off in single file. Arriving at Colerain too late to encounter the enemy, who a few hours before had raised the siege, they after a short pursuit returned home; and by no means allayed our apprehensions, by their fearful accounts of Indian warfare and savage barbarity. We had often heard of the cruelties practised by the Indians; but the details of the burning of Mr.

Abner Hunt, whom they had taken prisoner a few hours before their attack on the garrison, shocked us beyond measure. It is much easier to conceive than to describe the feelings of the garrison, when, after being urged and entreated by the wretched man to purchase their own safety, and, above all, his life, by surrendering to the enemy, they saw him led off, and witnessed the fearful preparations for torture; or, the heart-sickening anguish of hope suddenly extinguished, the mute despair of the prisoner, as he heard the decided, though reluctant refusal of the garrison, to save his life at the certain loss of their own. The Indians had tied their prisoner to a sapling within sight of the garrison, who distinctly heard his screams, and built a large fire so near as to scorch him, inflicting the most acute pain; then, as his flesh from the action of the fire, and the frequent application of live coals, became less sensible, making deep incisions in his limbs, as if to renew his susceptibility of pain; answering his cries for water to allay the extreme thirst caused by burning, by fresh tortures; and finally, when exhausted and fainting, death seemed approaching to release the wretched prisoner, terminating his sufferings by applying flaming brands to his naked bowels. In this siege, which lasted two days, the Indians suffered severely in killed and wounded, without inflicting any serious personal injury on the garrison; whose principal loss was in cattle, destroyed or driven off by the enemy. The attack on Dunlap's station was followed by successive depredations and murders by the Indians.

In the ensuing spring, they attacked several boats, killed many persons, and took some prisoners on the Ohio. Individuals were killed, or made prisoners, even on the outlots of Cincinnati, and near the mouth of Deer creek, and many were the "hair-breadth escapes" from captivity or death. It is but few years since, that near the turnpike, three miles above this city, might be seen the large elm, behind which some Indians stood concealed, and as he passed on horseback, seized and made —— Bailey prisoner : and not more than five miles beyond, where the same road crosses the narrows of Little Miami, only a few months since, I recognized the spot where the brave, but unfortunate Newell, fell a victim to the rifle and scalping knife of the savage.— The successful expedition of Gen. Scott, of Kentucky, against the Indians on the Wabash in May, 1791, had but little effect on the tribes north of us, whose boldness and daring remained unchecked. Early in the summer of that year they stole our horses, two in number, from a shed adjoining our cabin ; and only a few days afterward we narrowly escaped the total massacre of our family. We had just ended our evening's repast, and were about to rise from our table, when one of my sisters, hearing, as she believed, the almost noiseless tread of approaching footsteps, casting her eyes upon the door, and perceiving, as she thought, the latch gently rising, sprang up, and seizing it, held it down until the

doors were barred. Immediate preparations
were made for defence. Our lights were instantly
extinguished, and while the females of our family
sought safety by covering themselves with beds,
the men, three in number, with a rifle and two
muskets, manned the port holes above ; and by
frequently moving to the different sides of the
house, endeavoured to impress the Indians with
an idea of our strength. The tread of the Indians
was now distinctly heard, and the forms of two
or three of them were indistinctly seen gliding
through the darkness. Their intention no doubt,
had been to take us by surprise ; and opening
the back door silently, to have first fired upon
us, and then to have rushed into the house, and
with their tomahawks have completed the work
of destruction ; but failing in this, being too few
to take us by assault, seeing no opportunity of
injuring us, and probably too, not wishing to
alarm the town without first effecting some mischief, they soon stole off and disappeared. But
a few minutes, however, had elapsed before we
heard the crack of rifles within two hundred
yards of us, followed by the shrill war whoop of
the Indians. Three musket shots in quick succession soon sounded an alarm, and in ten minutes about thirty men had assembled at the
cabin of Ensign Bowman, on the hill side, a short
distance west of us. They found the family in
great consternation. The Indians had fired into
the house through an opening between the logs,
and guided by the light within, had wounded Mrs.
Bowman slightly in her body. At sunrise of the

following day a small party pursued the Indians, whose number from their trails did not exceed six ; and toward noon finding their tracks quite fresh, and judging that they were now almost in view of the enemy, moved cautiously, half bent, and straining their eyes as if they would look through every tree before them. Suddenly at the sharp crack of one of their own rifles, as by one impulse, each sprang behind a tree, waiting a few moments in breathless suspense the appearance of the Indians. At this moment a huge bear was seen bounding off a few rods from their left, and the disappointed marksman was heard muttering curses on his rifle for deceiving his expectations. The rest of the party, however, who had strong doubts of his courage, and believed that he had availed himself of this opportunity to avoid an encounter with the enemy, were deeply incensed ; and could with difficulty be prevented from anticipating the decision of a court martial, by inflicting summary punishment on the culprit, who, in one unlucky moment, as they confidently believed, had deprived them of the certain spoils of victory.

Soon after the failure of Col. Harmar's expedition, government had determined to send a powerful force against the Indians, sufficient at once to reduce them to subjection. Troops were daily arriving at Cincinnati, so that in September, 1791, a large force, consisting of regulars, levies, and militia, under the command of Gen. St. Clair, then governor of the north-western territory, was ready to march against the enemy.

From the known experience and distinguished reputation of the general as a soldier, and the character of the officers under his command, the greater part of whom had " seen service," complete success was confidently anticipated ; and in the full expectation that the Indians would soon be humbled into submission, and apprehending no danger while a force so formidable guarded their frontiers, the inhabitants of the Miami valley enjoyed for some weeks tranquillity and repose.

From Cincinnati, the march of Gen. St. Clair's army was in a direction a little west of north.— Passing Fort Hamilton, which they had previously built on the site of the present town of Hamilton, and crossing the Great Miami at that place, they advanced about twenty-six miles, and having built Fort St. Clair, near the present town of Eaton, marched twenty-two miles farther north, and erected Fort Jefferson.

Their progress unavoidably had been slow, not only from the delay of building forts, but from the nature of the ground over which they passed, where much labour was required in opening and making a road for the passage of their artillery and baggage wagons. They had suffered some detention too, from the want of supplies ; sometimes failing from the neglect of contractors, and at others, interrupted or cut off by the enemy. Pursuing the direct course to the Indian villages on the Maumee River, or Miami of Lake Erie, they had on the 3d of November advanced about thirty miles north-westwardly of Fort Jefferson,

and within forty-five miles of the nearest town of
the enemy; while the inhabitants of the Miami
settlements, who had almost daily heard of the
progress of the army, and who confidently anticipated their complete success, were anxiously
expecting soon to hear that they had achieved a
glorious and decisive victory.   But inexpressible
was their disappointment, and deep was their
consternation, when on the evening of the 6th of
November accounts reached them of the total
defeat of the army; accounts confirmed every
hour by some of its fugitives, with more fearful
details of Indian barbarity, and followed almost
immediately by the broken remains of the army,
who marching night and day reached Cincinnati
on the 8th.   The battle of the 4th of November,
1791, and the disastrous defeat of Gen. St.
Clair's army, form a part of the early history of
the west; most of their details have been told,
and need not here be repeated.   I may, however,
be allowed to state some facts not generally
known, related by officers who were in that en-
gagement; and others communicated to me afterward, while a captive among the Indians, by
prisoners taken in that battle.

On the afternoon of the 3d November, the
main body of the army, principally regulars and
levies, encamped on the south side of a branch
of the Wabash, in two lines, distant from each
other seventy or eighty yards, fronting the stream
and extending along it, and within a few hundred
feet of it, about three hundred and fifty yards.
On the north side of the stream, and a quarter

of a mile in advance of the main army, the militia under Col. Oldham were posted; and beyond them at a suitable distance, an advance guard of a company of regulars under Captain Slough, was placed. Some time before light of the ensuing day, the approach of the Indians in considerable numbers compelled this guard to fall back upon the militia. But although this fact was reported to Gen. Butler, and although he was advised that an attack would certainly be made upon the army that morning, he seemed to have either regarded the information "as an idle tale," or to have relied so confidently in the strength of the army as to have considered it invincible.

The morning of the 4th had dawned; the shrill fife and rolling drum had sounded the cheerful reveille; the troops, as was their daily practice, had manned their lines, and stood under arms in battle array until after the sun had risen, when no enemy appearing, they had retired, some to prepare their breakfasts or perform various other duties, and not a few to lounge in their tents.— Suddenly the sharp crack of a thousand rifles, mingled with the hideous and deafening yells of the Indians, announced but too certainly that the militia in front were attacked in great force by the enemy. The drums of the encampment instantly beat to arms, and the soldiers hastened to their posts; but scarcely had the troops formed and prepared for action, when the routed militia, closely pursued by the savages, rushed through the front line into the camp, throwing that line into a confusion from which it could not be entirely recovered. Following up their advantage, the Indians boldly advanced upon the front, as if determined to force it, but meeting with a firm resistance, and receiving several well-directed volleys from our men, were compelled to fall back. Our troops now for a short time fought bravely, but contending under great disadvantages against superior numbers, soon became disheartened. Occupying an elevated piece of ground, while they stood openly exposed to the destructive fire of the Indians from behind trees and logs, their own principally passed entirely over the enemy; their bullets, and particularly the balls of their cannon, being afterward found lodged in the bodies and limbs of the trees thirty feet above the ground. Early in the action the troops were entirely surrounded by the Indians, who, while some of them retreated from one side of the camp before the charge of the bayonet, others rushed in on the opposite side, or on the flanks, killing and scalping the wounded. These charges were repeated several times, but always with great loss to our troops; indeed it seemed as if the Indians fled at first before their charge as if to draw them out some distance from their lines, then suddenly turning upon them, compel them to retreat, leaving their wounded to certain destruction. It was during one of these charges, that the brave, but unfortunate Gen. Butler was killed. He had been mortally wounded early in the battle and carried to his tent; and, determining to sell his life as dearly as possible, was there placed in a reclining posture, with a pair of pistols by his side.   In pursuing our troops, retreating in their turn, two warriors at once espied him, and both anxious to plunder his person, as well as to take his scalp, rushed forward ; the one only a few feet in advance of the other.—The foremost Indian had but just entered his tent, when the general, levelling one pistol, shot him dead ; but while in the act of presenting the second, received the stroke of the hurled tomahawk of the other, and instantly expired.   A few rods from this tent, Capt. Ford, the only surviving officer of artillery, severely wounded and disabled, was providentially saved from a similar fate, by having been placed against a large tree on the opposite side from that on which the Indians were then charging.   The fatal rifles of the enemy were still dealing death, and their tomahawks and scalping knives completing the work of destruction, had killed nearly half the soldiers, and more than three fourths of the officers, when Gen. St. Clair, satisfied that farther resistance would be hopeless, determined on a retreat as the only means of saving the remnant of the army. The remaining troops were now formed under Col. Darke, and vigorously charging the Indians, who gave way on their right and left, gained the road and commenced a retreat, which soon increased to a flight.   Not only were the artillery and baggage abandoned, but even the wounded, with very few exceptions, were left to their fate. Each struggling for his own preservation, thought not of the safety of others.   The life of Capt.

Ford, however, was saved by the devoted attachment of one of his men, who, placing him upon a horse, bore him safely from the battle ground; while Dr. Richard Allison, senior surgeon of the army, than whom few were more brave, humane, and benevolent, mounted on his own powerful and spirited horse, with his waiter seated behind him, brought off from the field Capt. Shaylor, and three others, who, laying hold of the mane and tail of the noble animal, were enabled to escape the pursuit of the enemy. Of about fifteen hundred men who engaged in battle on that fatal morning, six hundred and thirty, including thirty-seven officers, were killed; and two hundred and forty-four, including thirty officers, were wounded. Beside these, a number of pack-horsemen, wagoners, and others attached to the army, were killed; and of nearly two hundred women, principally its followers, three only escaped; about fifty were killed, and the residue were made prisoners. Had the Indians pursued their advantage, they might easily have cut off the whole remnant of the troops, many of whom, soon after the retreat commenced, threw away their arms, betaking themselves to flight. But having signally defeated the army, and satiated for a time their thirst for carnage, the greater part of them remained to plunder the camp; while those who pursued the flying troops, cutting off the stragglers and scalping the wounded, after following them about four miles, fearing they should not obtain their share of the spoil, suddenly gave over the pursuit and returned to the encampment.—

Here, after plundering and stripping the dead, securing every thing that they could individually appropiate to themselves, and after being gorged with feasting, principally on slaughtered bullocks, they began to drink and carouse; and while some became stupid, others growing more ferocious as they felt the influence of the "fire water," rent the air with their hideous war whoops, acted over their savage feats, cutting and mangling the dead bodies; and finding many not yet dead from their wounds, tore out the hearts of some and throwing others into the fire terminated their sufferings. A few Indians less ferocious, dressing themselves in the uniforms of the dead officers, strutted about the encampment. One of these I afterward saw, while a prisoner among the Shawnees, wearing the dress coat of a field officer of infantry, with silver epauletts on his shoulders, and a watch suspended from each ear. With one hand taking hold of the facing of his coat, he said to me, "Me kill um;" and with the other smiting his breast, vociferated, "Captain Walker! Great man me!!" The Indians were led by several brave and experienced chiefs; and beside the infamous renegade Girty, and the notorious Col. Elliot, I was told that Captain M'Kee of the royal Americans, and several of the British officers, were in the battle.

The defeat of Gen. St. Clair was not followed by those disastrous consequences which at first were apprehended. Strong garrisons being kept up at Hamilton, St. Clair, and even Fort Jefferson, afforded to the inhabitants of the Miami settlements great protection; while in Fort Washington, several companies of troops, more than were necessary for its defence, not only gave constant security to the citizens of Cincinnati, but the means of repelling any inroads of the enemy, and of extending aid in case of attack, to other villages.

CHAPTER III.

Cincinnati in 1791—Public worship on the Sabbath with military accompaniments—Privations of the first settlers—Early spring of 1791-2—Celebration of the 4th of July at Fort Washington, and capture of Spencer by the Indians.

FEW only of those who now behold Cincinnati, in point of extent, population, and the number, beauty, and permanency of its buildings, the seventh city in the United States, have any correct idea of what it was more than forty-three years since. About the 22d of February, 1791, when I first saw it, it contained not more than forty dwellings, all log cabins, and not exceeding two hundred and fifty inhabitants. In the southeastern part of the town, near the site of his present dwelling, stood the cabin of Mr. D. E. Wade, in the midst of the forest trees; and just below on the first bank, between the mouth of Deer creek and Lawrence-street, were scattered among the trees, four or five more cabins.— Between Eastern-row (a narrow street now enlarged into Broadway) and Main-street, on Front

and Columbia streets, there were about twenty
log houses; and on Sycamore and Main, principally on the second bank, or hill, as it was called,
there were scattered about fifteen cabins more.
At the foot of this bank, extending across Broadway and Main streets, were large ponds, on
which as lately as the winter of 1798, I have
seen boys skating. All the ground from the foot
of the second bank to the river, between Lawrence-street and Broadway, and appropriated to
the fort, was an open space, on which, although
no trees were left standing, most of their large
trunks were still lying. On the top, and about
eighty feet distant from the brow of the second
bank, facing the river, stood Fort Washington,
occupying nearly all the ground between Third
and Fourth streets, and between Ludlow-street
and Broadway. This fort, of nearly a square
form, was simply a wooden fortification, whose
four sides or walls, each about one hundred and
eighty feet long, were constructed of hewed logs,
erected into barracks two stories high, connected
at the corners by high pickets, with bastions or
block houses, also of hewed logs, and projecting
about ten feet in front of each side of the fort, so
that the cannon placed within them could be
brought to rake its walls. Through the centre
of the south side, or front of the fort, was the
principal gateway, a passage through this line of
barracks, about twelve feet wide and ten feet
high, secured by strong wooden doors of the same
dimensions. Appended to the fort on its north
side, and enclosed with high palisades extending

from its north-east and north-west corners to a
block house, was a small triangular space, in
which were constructed shops for the accommodation of the artificers. Extending along the
whole front of the fort, was a fine esplanade,
about eighty feet wide and enclosed with a handsome paling on the brow of the bank ; the descent
from which to the lower bottom was sloping, about
thirty feet. The front and sides of the fort were
whitewashed, and at a small distance, presented
a handsome and imposing appearance. On the
eastern side, were the officers' gardens, finely
cultivated, ornamented with beautiful summer
houses, and yielding in their season an abundance
of vegetables.

The 22d of February, 1791, was celebrated
by the officers at Fort Washington, with their
ladies, and those of Columbia and Cincinnati, together about twelve, by what was then in the west
considered a splendid ball ; preceded by the
firing of cannon, the discharge of rockets, and
the exhibition of a variety of fire works ; and in
riding, visiting, dancing, and other amusements
of the winter, they soon forgot their wounds, and
the dangers of their late disastrous campaign.

Often as I sit securely in the house of God,
the spacious temple of the Most High, surveying
the hundreds that surround me fearlessly raising
their notes of praise, and tranquilly worshipping
the Father of mercies, the days of other years,
and scenes long, long past, recur to my mind
with all the vividness of recent occurrence. Then
fresh in my remembrance is the rude log house,

the first humble sanctuary of the first settlers of
Columbia, standing amidst the tall forest trees,
on the beautiful knoll, where now may be seen
a grave yard, and the ruins of a Baptist meeting
house of later years. There, on the holy Sabbath, we were wont to assemble to hear the word
of life; but our fathers met with their muskets
and rifles, prepared for action, and ready to repel
any attack of the enemy. And while the
watchman on the walls of Zion was uttering his
faithful and pathetic warning, the sentinels without, at a few rods distance, with measured step,
were now pacing their walks, and now standing
and with strained eyes endeavouring to pierce
through the distance, carefully scanning every
object that seemed to have life or motion.

The first clergyman I there heard preach was
Mr. Gano, father of the late Gen. Gano of this
city, then a captain, and one of the earliest
settlers of Columbia. Never shall I forget that
holy and venerable man, with locks white with
years, as with a voice tremulous with age, he ably
expounded the word of truth, and affectionately
encouraged penitent sinners to hope in the Divine
forgiveness, from the words of Job, "O that I
knew where I might find him! that I might
come even to his seat! I would order my cause
before him, and fill my mouth with arguments."
He has long since gone to reap the reward of them
"that turn many to righteousness," and most of
those, once his hearers, are dwellers in that land,
whence they shall never emigrate. Often too,
as I rest quietly in a comfortable dwelling, or sit

at a table crowned with plenty, possessing not only every necessary, but some of the luxuries of life, I think of the hardships of the early settlers of the west; and contrasting their perils and privations with the security and plenty of the present day, mentally exclaim with the psalmist, "The lines are fallen unto us in pleasant places; yea, we have a goodly heritage." My wife, who now sits beside me, and whose parents settled at Marietta in the spring of 1790, says that so great in that summer was the scarcity of bread stuffs, that her mother was obliged to send her children from the house, while she prepared bread for her boarders, who by some fortunate circumstance had obtained a bushel of corn meal; and I have often heard, that in the Miami settlements the same summer, many, while planting and tending their crops, were confined wholly to boiled corn, as a substitute for bread; and, sometimes destitute even of that, used in its stead a sweet bulbous root, called bear grass.

I well recollect, that in 1791, so scarce and dear was flour, that the little that could be afforded in families, was laid by to be used only in sickness, or for the entertainment of friends; and although corn was then abundant, there was but one (Wickerham's) a floating mill on the Little Miami, near where Turpin's now stands. Built in a small flat boat tied to the bank, its wheel turning slowly with the natural current running between the flat and a small pirogue anchored in the stream, and on which one end of its shaft rested; and having only one pair of small

stones, it was at best barely sufficient to supply
meal for the inhabitants of Columbia, and the
neighbouring families; and sometimes, from low
water, and other unfavourable circumstances, it
was of little use, so that we were obliged to supply the deficiency from hand mills, a most labo-
rious mode of grinding.

The winter of 1791-2, was followed by an
early and delightful spring; indeed I have often
thought that our first western winters were much
milder, our springs earlier, and our autumns
longer than they now are. On the last of
February, some of the trees were putting forth
their foliage; in March, the redbud, the haw-
thorn, and the dogwood, in full bloom, checkered
the hills, displaying their beautiful colours of rose
and lily; and in April, the ground was covered
with may apple, bloodroot, ginseng, violets, and
a great variety of herbs and flowers. Flocks of
parroquets were seen, decked in their rich plu-
mage of green and gold. Birds of various
species, and of every hue, were flitting from tree
to tree, and the beautiful redbird, and the un-
taught songster of the west, made the woods vocal
with their melody. Now might be heard the
plaintive wail of the dove, and now the rumbling
drum of the partridge, or the loud gobble of the
turkey. Here might be seen the clumsy bear,
doggedly moving off, or urged by pursuit into a
labouring gallop, retreating to his citadel in the
top of some lofty tree; or approached suddenly,
raising himself erect in the attitude of defence,
facing his enemy and waiting his approach; there

the timid deer, watchfully resting, or cautiously feeding, or aroused from his thicket, gracefully bounding off, then stopping, erecting his stately head, and for a moment gazing around, or snuffing the air to ascertain his enemy, instantly springing off, clearing logs and bushes at a bound, and soon distancing his pursuers. It seemed an earthly paradise; and but for apprehension of the wily copperhead, who lay silently coiled among the leaves or beneath the plants, waiting to strike his victim; the horrid rattle snake, who more chivalrous, however, with head erect amidst his ample folds, prepared to dart upon his foe, generously with the loud noise of his rattle, apprised him of danger; and the still more fearful and insidious savage, who, crawling upon the ground, or noiselessly approaching behind trees and thickets, sped the deadly shaft or fatal bullet, you might have fancied you were in the confines of Eden or the borders of Elysium.

At this delightful season, the inhabitants of our village went forth to their labour, inclosing their fields, which the spring flood had opened, tilling their ground, and planting their corn for their next year's sustenance. I said, went forth, for their principal corn field was distant from Columbia about one and a half miles east, and adjoining the extensive plain on which the town stood.— That large tract of alluvial ground, still known by the name of Turkey Bottom, and which, lying about fifteen feet below the adjoining plain, and annually overflowed, is yet very fertile, was laid off into lots of five acres each, and owned

3

by the inhabitants of Columbia; some possessing
one, and others two or more lots; and to save
labour, was inclosed with one fence. Here the
men generally worked in companies, exchanging
labour, or in adjoining fields, with their fire arms
near them, that in case of an attack they might
be ready to unite for their common defence.—
Here, their usual annual crop of corn from
ground very ordinarily cultivated, was eighty
bushels per acre; and some lots well tilled produced a hundred, and in very favourable seasons,
a hundred and ten bushels to the acre. An inhabitant of New-England, New-Jersey, or some
portions of Maryland, would scarcely think it
credible, that in hills four feet apart, were four
or five stalks, one and a half inches in diameter,
and fifteen feet in height, bearing each two or
three ears of corn, of which some were so far
from the ground, that to pull them, an ordinary
man was obliged to stand on tiptoe. Small as I
then was, I drove the oxen, while my father, followed by the corn dressers, guided the plough
between the rows; for having lost our horses,
we were obliged to substitute cattle, which, however, connected by a long yoke having the draft
near to one of them, and permitting each to walk
in a separate row, fully supplied the place of a
horse.

Well do I recollect with what alacrity I performed my labour, on the promise of my father,
that I should spend the approaching fourth of
July at Fort Washington; and well do I remember with what gayety and high expectations of

coming pleasure, I left home to realize those expectations. It was on the afternoon of the 3d July, 1792, in company with my sisters, and several ladies of Columbia, and some officers who had arrived there on the morning of that day, for the express purpose of conveying them to Fort Washington, to partake of a dinner to be given by the officers, and followed with a ball on the evening of the fourth. We left the shore in front of my father's dwelling, in a fine barge rowed by eight soldiers, and were soon descending with the rapid current of the river, at the rate of six miles an hour. The scenery of the Ohio between Columbia and Cincinnati was in those days truly romantic ; scarcely a tree had been cut on either side, between the mouth of Crawfish and that of Deer creek, a distance of more than four miles. The sandbar now extending from its left bank, opposite to Sportsman's Hall, was then a small island, between which and the Kentucky shore was a narrow channel, with sufficient depth of water for the passage of boats. The upper and lower points of this island were bare, but its centre, embracing about four acres, was covered with small cotton wood, and surrounded by willows extending along its sides almost down to the water's edge. The right bank of the river, crowned with its lofty hills, now gradually ascending, and now rising abruptly to their summits, and forming a vast amphitheatre, was from Columbia, extending down about two miles, very steep, and covered with trees quite down to the beach. From thence, nearly opposite the foot of the island, its ascent became more gradual, and for two miles farther down, bordering the tall trees with which it was covered, was a thick growth of willows, through which in many places it was difficult to penetrate. Below this, the beach was wide and stony, with only here and there a small tuft of willows, while the wood on the side and on the top of the bank was more open. Not far from this bank and near the line of the present turnpike, was a narrow road leading from Columbia to Cincinnati, just wide enough for the passage of a wagon, which, winding round the point of the hill above Deer creek, descended northwardly about four hundred feet, and crossing that creek, and in a southerly direction ascending gradually its western bank, led along the ground, now Symme's-street, directly toward Fort Washington, and diverging at the intersection of Lawrence-street to the right and left of the fort, entered the town. I have been thus particular in describing the river between Columbia and Cincinnati, not only that those who now see it, may have some idea of its former appearance, but that the reader may better understand the narrative that follows.

Scarcely an hour, enlivened by conversation, had elapsed from the time we left Columbia, before we landed on the shore in front of the garrison, and ascending the bank, in a few minutes entered Fort Washington.

The morning of the 4th was ushered in with the discharge of thirteen rounds from the cannon of the fort; at twelve the firing was repeated, and the troops under arms performed various evolutions; at dinner, as usual, the toasts were followed by the discharge of artillery; at dusk there was a brilliant exhibition of fireworks; and at night, if not a splendid, yet, in the opinion of those present, a very agreeable and sprightly ball. The two succeeding days were spent by me in various amusements; but having exhausted these, and grown tired of play, I became restless and uneasy, and determining to return home, with all the inconsiderateness of childhood (for I was not then eleven years old,) secretly left the garrison, whose first knowledge of my absence was the report of my capture. Reaching the bank in front of the fort about three o'clock on the afternoon of the 7th, I found a canoe, with four persons on board, bound for Columbia, just about to push off from the shore. Discovering one of them to be an acquaintance, I hailed them, requesting them to take me on board; which request, after a few moments consultation, they complied with. The canoe, which was small, narrow, and quite unsteady, had proceeded only a few rods above the mouth of Deer creek, when one of the men, much intoxicated, having made several lurches on both sides, at length tumbling overboard, and nearly oversetting us, after a few awkward flounces reached the shore. Not knowing how to swim, and being afraid to continue in the canoe, I prevailed with the remaining men to set me on shore; when, after a few minutes, leaving the drunken man sitting on the bank, we proceeded

toward Columbia. In the bow of the canoe stood
Mr. Jacob Light, and with a pole aided in pro-
pelling it; in the stern, a stranger, a swarthy,
athletic man, with thick black, bushy hair, sat
with a paddle, which he sometimes used as an
oar, and at others as a rudder; and in the bottom
of its centre sat Mrs. Coleman, then an old woman of sixty. For myself, I walked along the
beach, a little below the canoe, now listening to
the merry conversation of my companions, and
now amusing myself by skimming small flat
stones over the surface of the water. About a
mile above the mouth of Deer creek, a canoe,
which we had discovered some time before descending the middle of the river, having on board
some market people, and a woman, whose child
cried loudly and incessantly, passed us, and eli-
cited from the old lady, as is common in such
cases, some remarks on the government of children. We had rounded the point of a small cove,
less than a mile below the foot of the island, and
proceeded a few hundred yards along the close
willows, here bordering the beach at about two
rods' distance from the water, when the stranger
in the stern of the canoe looking back, and discovering the drunken man staggering along the
shore, nearly a mile below us, remarked, with an
oath, that he would be "bait for the Indians."
Scarcely had he spoken, and resumed his labour,
for a few moments suspended, when turning my
eyes from the drunken man to the men in the
canoe, I saw Mr. Light spring suddenly into the
river, and the stranger at the stern falling over

toward the shore. In the next moment, hearing the sharp crack of two rifles in instant succession, and looking toward the willows, about two rods above me, I saw, through the thick smoke of their guns, two Indians, with faces black as midnight, rushing toward the canoe. Never shall I forget my feelings at that moment. For an instant I stood motionless, and my brief reflection in that moment, as I involuntarily drew down my head between my shoulders, was, *I have made some narrow escapes, but now death is inevitable.* One Indian was now within ten feet of me; in his right hand was the uplifted tomahawk, and in his left the naked scalping knife. Instantly, as on wheeling, I ran toward the water, hoping to reach the canoe and push out into the river: he passed above me down to the shore, near which I arrived just at the moment when, striking his tomahawk into the head of the unfortunate stranger, seizing him by the hair, passing his knife quickly around the scalp, and tearing it violently off, he held it up for a moment with fiendish exultation. Finding I could not gain the canoe, which by this time had got out into the current, turning from the heart-sickening sight of the mangled man, and dreading every moment a similar fate, I next attempted to run down the river, in the vain hope of escaping; but I had not proceeded ten steps, when the other Indian, discovering my design, easily headed me. Instead, however, of seizing me violently, approaching within a few feet, he extended to me his hand, in token of peace. I took it, and from

what I had heard of the character and customs
of Indians, feeling assured of present safety, became at once calm. The whole of these events
did not occupy more than thirty seconds. The
Indians had been on the hill in quest of horses,
when hearing the loud crying of the child in the
canoe that about ten minutes before had passed
us, they came down to the bank of the river,
thinking they might have an opportunity of
effecting some mischief. Arriving too late to
injure those in that canoe, and discovering ours
about a quarter of a mile below, the Indians
determined to wait our approach; and having
planned to kill the men and woman, and take me
a prisoner, concealed themselves behind a large
log among the willows, whence, as we came
nearly opposite, they made their attack.

I had time only to cast a brief glance at the
shocking scene before me; to see Mr. Light,
who, although wounded in the left arm, was with
his right swimming out into the river, about a
hundred yards from shore; the dead body of the
stranger lying just in the edge of the water;
Mrs. Coleman about two rods out in the river,
her clothes spread over the water, and with her
head near its surface, apparently floating, and
the desolate canoe slowly descending with the
current, when the Indian who had taken me prisoner, and who still held my hand, led me off;
and followed by his companion, whose tomahawk
was extended almost over my head, soon began
to climb the high hill bordering the Ohio.

Crossing the road a short distance, we stopped

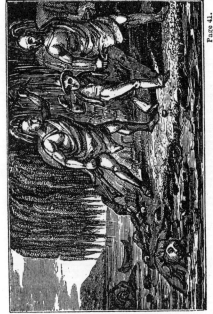

SPENCER TAKEN PRISONER.

Page 41.

a few moments on the hill's side ; the Indians, casting their keen glances around them, and listening intently as if hearing some sound indicative of danger, then, apparently satisfied that they were undiscovered, resumed their retreat, and quickly gaining the top of the hill, ran off in a northerly direction at the height of my speed, one of them still holding me by my hand, the other following with his uplifted tomahawk.

Having run, as I judged, about four miles, discovering my feet bare, (for I had soon after leaving Cincinnati thrown my shoes into the canoe,) my conductor, whom I now regarded as my master, supplied me with a pair of moccasons, and seemed much pleased when in return for them I gave him my pocket handkerchief, which he received as a mark of gratitude. To the other Indian, who had now put his tomahawk in his belt, fearing I might have excited his jealousy, I presented my hat, which at first, as worthless, he dashed on the ground ; then, instantly picking it up, thinking, no doubt, it might direct pursuit, carried it in his hand until evening, when he burned it. Relaxing our speed, (although the long strides of the Indians kept me in a continual trot,) and still pursuing a northerly course, about an hour before sunset, descending a high hill, we reached a small stream, running in a westerly direction, and which I have since believed to be the rivulet and the hill adjoining Sharon. Entering this stream, we waded up it about half a mile, the leading Indian directing me to step in his track, while the other followed treading in mine; then leaving it, and travelling about a mile farther north, encamped at sunset on a low point of thick underwood, near a rivulet. Here, while one Indian kindled a fire, the other went in pursuit of game, and soon returning with a raccoon, which he had killed with his rifle, proceeded to dress it by singeing off the hair, then dividing it, broiled it on the fire. The Indians ate voraciously, but, being exceedingly weary, I could eat very little ; beside, I had just witnessed a most sickening scene, calculated, for a time, to destroy all relish for food. While my captor was dressing the raccoon for supper, I had seen the other Indian, whom I shall now call by his name, Waw-pawwawquaw, or White Loon, drawing from its sheath his large brass-handled knife, and cutting off the limb of a small grub, near the body, take from his bullet pouch the black scalp recently torn from the head of the unfortunate white man, and cutting a small hole near its edge, and hanging it on the stump of the severed limb, deliberately and carefully scrape off the thick fat ; then forming a small hoop about six inches in diameter, with a thread of deer's sinew, stretch the scalp within it, as if he had been preparing to dry the skin of an animal. Having finished their meal, the Indians prepared for rest; first tying the middle of a cord around my neck, and extending its ends around my wrists separately, they spread a blanket on the ground, and ordered me to lie down ; then, lying down on each side of me, passing the ends of the cord under their bodies, and covering themselves with the remaining blanket, soon sunk into a profound sleep.

For some time I lay ruminating on the sad events of the past day; my mind now filled with fearful apprehensions of the future, and now "stung with the thought of home," to which I feared I should never return. Here, as I thought of my beloved parents and affectionate sisters, and felt for the moment that I should never again behold them, tears of bitter regret flowed plentifully, and scarcely could I repress my sobs; then, as for a moment a ray of hope shone through the gloom, my soul became more tranquil, and I began to revolve in my mind the means and the probabilities of escape; overcome at length with fatigue, in deep sleep I soon forgot all my sorrows.

CHAPTER IV.

Mrs. Coleman floats down the river to Cincinnati, and gives information of Spencer's captivity—The captors take their course toward the Shawnee villages —A hurricane—Spencer makes his escape from the Indians, and lodges under a fallen tree.

To me it has ever seemed almost incredible, that Mrs. Coleman, after jumping out of the canoe into the river, should have floated quite down to Cincinnati, and there, being taken out of the water, have communicated the bloody event of that day, and the news of my captivity;

but the fact has been often declared by herself,
and asserted by others of undoubted veracity,
some of whom it is said had aided in saving her.
I have been told, however, that the first news of
my captivity was communicated by Mr. Light,
who, on seeing the Indians retreat, swam to the
shore, and making the best of his way to Fort
Washington, reported the fact. The commanding officer immediately despatched an express
to my father, announcing the painful occurrence,
and proposing to send out a small force of
regulars. While the news was spreading, a
number of the inhabitants of Columbia soon
assembled, prepared, and anxious to pursue the
Indians; but my father apprehending, that finding themselves pursued, and unable to carry me
off, the Indians would instantly kill me, returned
by the express a request that no troops should be
sent after them; then, with some difficulty, dis-
suading his neighbours from their purposed pursuit, obtained their promise that they would proceed no farther than the spot where the dead man
still lay, and where I was taken prisoner. To describe the feelings of my parents when the news of
my captivity reached them, would for me be impossible. To be bereaved of an only son, and the
youngest of a once numerous family, of whom
but six were living, would by death, under ordinary circumstances, have been a severe affliction.
Had I been found dead, inhumanly scalped and
mangled, on the beech, by the side of my unfortunate companion, the shock, though powerful,
would have gradually subsided, and the violence

of grief would with time have abated ; but, that I should be carried away captive by the Indians, the cruel barbarous savages, was to my parents, and especially to my mother, almost insupportable. Often, when she thought of me, she fancied she saw me fainting with fatigue, or famishing with hunger, or pining with disease ; and sometimes her terrified imagination represented me falling by the knife, or sinking under the stroke of the tomahawk, or expiring at the stake in the flames, under the most cruel tortures. Nor was she relieved from these distressing apprehensions and this painful state of suspense, until some time in November following my captivity, when certain information was received from the commanding officer at Post Vincennes, that I was then living, and had been seen at the Indian village, near the mouth of Auglaize, only a few weeks before, by the late Captain Wells, (Indian agent, who was killed by the Indians at the capture of Chicago, in the late war with Great Britain,) then a prisoner at large among the Indians.

With the dawn of the morning of the 8th of July, the Indians awoke, and untying the cord with which I was bound, we all arose. Our scanty breakfast was soon made from the remains of the raccoon which had furnished our supper ; our baggage, consisting of two blankets, a bridle, a cord, and a scalp, was shouldered, the priming of the rifles was examined, and before the sun arose we were marching in single file, my master in front, myself in the centre,

and the White Loon bringing up the rear, in the
direct course of the Shawnee villages. The
morning of this day was very pleasant ; the sky
was clear, and the air balmy and refreshing ;
the ground, less broken and hilly, was covered
with verdure ; the tall woods through which we
passed were beautiful, and but for the condition
in which I was, a captive, whose every step
bore him farther from friends and home, I
should have been delighted. As it was, however, my mind by degrees became more cheerful, and my spirits began to resume their native
elasticity. About noon this day, passing along
the east side of a hill, beyond which there appeared to be a large opening, the Indians moved
cautiously, half bent, and with trailed rifles.
Proceeding about half a mile, we halted in a
deep ravine ; when White Loon, taking the
bridle and pursuing a westerly course down the
hollow, soon disappeared. In about ten minutes,
however, he returned, mounted on a fine cream-
coloured horse, which he had just stolen, and
taking me up behind him, trotted off several
miles, the other Indian following, until coming
to a thick undergrowth, we slackened our pace
into a brisk walk. Here we found a faint trace,
which, pursuing a few miles, led us into a plain
path, which I afterward learned was the Indians'
war path.

The Indians seemed highly pleased with their
late acquisition, riding, by turns, the spirited
animal, and occasionally taking me behind them
greatly relieved me from fatigue. But, alas !

how uncertain are the comforts of this world! about the middle of the afternoon the horse suddenly became dull, and seemingly sullen, so that with difficulty he could be urged forward. At length he stopped short, when in vain did the White Loon, on foot, apply the hickory: the horse only stood and kicked. In vain did the other Indian, dismounting, endeavour to lead him forward; he would proceed no farther. He had been violently attacked with either bots or cholic, and now lying suddenly down began to roll and groan, sometimes struggling with every limb, and sometimes dashing his head against the ground. The Indians stood over him, now beating him severely, and now talking to him in Indian, as if expostulating with him, or threatening him with vengeance in case of his remaining stubborn; at length my master, seizing his rifle as if to shoot him, began, in broken English, to curse him, and after loading the poor animal with all the opprobrious epithets he could think of, left him lying in the path. We encamped this evening about sunset, in a low rich bottom, near a beautiful stream; where, having made a fire, and roasted part of a young fawn, which White Loon a few minutes before had killed, we ate a very hearty supper, though without salt or bread, neither of which did we taste until we arrived at the Indian villages. After supper, taking a small piece of tobacco, and cutting it fine by passing the edge of his knife between his forefinger and thumb, receiving it as thus prepared into the palm of his left hand, the White Loon, with great solemnity and apparent devotion, sprinkled a few grains of it on the coals, an offering, as I afterward understood, to the Great Spirit, moving his lips as if uttering some petition ; then mingling the residue with some dried sumach leaves which he drew from his bullet pouch, and filling the bowl of his tomahawk, serving as a pipe, first smoked a few whiffs, then handed the pipe to his companion, who also smoking a few moments, returned it ; the Indians thus alternately puffing until the tobacco was consumed, frequently filling their mouths with smoke, and forcing it through their nostrils, closing their brief use of the pipe with a peculiar suck of the breath, and slight grinding of the teeth. The day had been remarkably fine ; we had travelled with short intermissions from early dawn until sunset, a distance of at least forty miles ; and very weary, myself at least, we lay down before our fire under a spreading beech, and soon fell into a profound sleep.

But we had slept only a few hours, when we were awakened by the roar of a tremendous hurricane passing only a few rods north of us, prostrating the trees with a terrible crash, and carrying devastation in its broad track. Over our heads the thunders broke with deafening peals, and the lightnings seemed a constant sheet of flame, when from the black dense cloud that was furiously sweeping eastward, it sent its vivid bolts athwart and onward, passing the storm with the rapidity of thought. I had sprung from the ground, and gazing on the awful

scene, stood motionless with terror. I feared
that the " great day of God's wrath was come,"
and I felt that I was not " able to stand ;" I
vowed to God that if he would spare me I would
dedicate to him my future life ; but, alas ! no
sooner had the fury of the storm passed, and the
thunder, now distant, ceased to terrify me, than
my vows to God were forgotten, and the thoughts
of the great white throne were banished. Expecting every moment to perish, I had stood for
some minutes unconscious of the presence of a
human being ; but, my terror a little subsiding,
looking at the Indians who were standing near
me, I saw them perfectly calm, apparently insen-
sible of danger, gazing with a sort of delighted
wonder ; and, frequently, as from the dense
cloud shot some more vivid bolt, with more
deafening peal, expressing their admiration
with their customary exclamation, Wawhaugh!
waugh ! On the morning of the 9th, the sun
arose brightly above the cloudless horizon, and
shone upon a sky as clear and beautiful as if
it had never been darkened by clouds or torn by
tempests ; and but for the bent tree tops above
us, the fallen branches around us, and the wide-
spread devastation before us, one would scarcely
have believed that in the heavens now so bright
and tranquil, desolation and terror had so lately
held their empire.

Breakfasting early, we pursued our journey ;
but our progress for the first half hour was slow,
and very difficult, having sometimes to climb over
the large bodies of the fallen trees, or to wind

around their uptorn roots; and sometimes to creep through their tops, interwoven with the underwood. One who has never seen the effects of a tornado can have but a faint idea of its power and operation. Here, for at least a quarter of a mile in width, and many miles in length, not a tree had been able to withstand its force; not only were the largest trees torn up by the roots, but many, one, and even two feet in diameter, were twisted off, some near to the ground, and others ten or twenty feet from it, apparently with as much ease as a man would break off a slender twig. Passing at length the fallen trees, and travelling on a few hours, on hearing the sound of a bell, we halted not far from a small opening on our left. Here Waw-pawwawquaw left us, again taking a westerly direction, and in about half an hour returned with an old black horse, probably a pack horse belonging to the army, that had given out, and afterward strayed off. Suspended from his neck, by a broad leather strap, was a large bell, which was now stuffed with grass to prevent its tinkling. This horse, though very far inferior to the one we had lost, was esteemed a valuable acquisition, particularly by me; for my feet had now become sore from walking, and I was delighted with the opportunity of relief which riding afforded. Mounted upon the old horse, a natural pacer, I now rode very pleasantly, enjoying the comfort, thus accidentally afforded me, without interruption; for the Indians seemed not at all disposed to share it with me. Having halted at

noon and taken some refreshment, we travelled
on until about six o'clock, when passing along
the side of a ridge into a low bottom, we stopped
on the south bank of a beautiful stream, (which
I have since been told by the White Loon is
Buck creek,) in the edge of a grove covering both
banks of the stream, skirting on one side a small
natural meadow of a few acres, and on the other
a large prairie extending a mile or two north and
west.   Here, determined to remain until the
next day, the Indians proceeded to hopple the
horse, and unstopping his bell, turned him out
to graze.   Next intending to secure me, they
ordered me to sit down with my back against a
small tree ; then taking their cord, tying it first
to the tree, passing it around my neck, and then
with a knot around my wrists separately, extending my arms obliquely on each side, they fastened
one end of it to a stake driven into the ground,
and the other to a root in the bank of the stream ;
then placing a large piece of bark over me to
shelter me from the sun, went out to hunt.
Being left alone, my thoughts alternately occupied with tender recollections of my home, and
a painful consciousness of my wretched condition ; sometimes revolving in my mind the pro-
bability of escape, then rejecting the thought as
chimerical, an hour had passed away.   I now
began to think seriously of making my escape,
and after a few minutes determined if possible
to effect it.   Being a firm believer in an over-
ruling Providence, and in the concern of God
for the welfare of his creatures, I first addressed

myself to him, and never did I utter a more sin-
cere and fervent prayer, supplicating his mercy
and imploring his aid ; and promising that if he
would deliver me from the hands of the savages,
and restore me to my beloved parents, I would
serve him the residue of my days " in truth with
all my heart." Believing, too, in the use of
means, I immediately began to exert my own
powers. Seizing the cord with which I was
bound, I first pulled it violently with my right
hand, attempting to break it, or detach it from
the root to which it was fastened ; failing in this
effort, I next laid hold of it with my left, endeavouring to pull down the stake to which it was
tied. While trying to effect this, looking at the
stake over my left hand, I discovered that the
cord was tied on the outside of the cuff of my
sleeve, and making the effort, succeeded in drawing my arm through it ; then, with the aid of my
left, disengaging my right hand in the same
way, I soon set myself entirely free. Picking
up the bridle, and thrusting in my bosom a small
piece of flyblown deer's meat as provision for
my journey, I soon found, bridled and unhoppled,
the old horse ; and mounting on his back, and
using the hopples (a cord of twisted bark) in
place of a whip, set off for home. From the
report of their rifles, which I had heard only a
few minutes before, I judged that the Indians
were about a mile off in a southwesterly direction,
and that I should easily return along the path
we had travelled, unperceived ; for considerate
for a child as I might have been, the thoughts

of home so engrossed my mind, that the proba-
bility and even certainty of pursuit did not enter
into my calculations, and I thought if I could
only get a few miles from the camp undiscovered, I should be safe. Unfortunately, as it
then seemed, I could not urge the horse beyond
a moderate pace. Whipping him with the
hopples until I was tired, I threw them down in
the path and supplied their place with a switch ;
but with all my exertions, striking with my
heels, jerking with the bridle, and applying the
switch simultaneously, I could not force him
into a trot. The sun, when I left the camp,
was about an hour high, and as I travelled
steadily until sunset, I had probably proceeded
three or four miles, when concluding to halt for
the night, I dismounted from the horse, and
bending a small twig by the side of the path in a
direction toward home, I led him a few hundred
yards directly off from the trace, up a gentle
slope of woodland, into a very close thicket of
small sassafras, and securing him with the bridle,
went in search of a lodging place.

About sixty yards south of the thicket, finding
a large fallen tree facing the path, and having
near its roots a hollow forming a shelter, I determined to lodge under it; but being very
hungry, and having no provision for my journey, saving a small piece of meat which I
thought I should more need on the morrow, I
concluded to make my evening's meal on raspberries, which grew here in great abundance. Stray-
ing from bush to bush, eagerly picking and eating

to satisfy my hunger, I paid little attention to
my course ; when, having eaten sufficiently, I
turned, as I thought, toward my lodging place,
but found, after walking some time, that I was
completely lost. I now felt greatly alarmed ;
I ran about in every direction, seeking the
thicket where I had tied the horse ; and terrified at the thought of perishing in the wilderness,
regretted for a moment my attempt to escape.
Happily, however, after wandering about for
some time, I found the log, and lying down
under it, pillowing my head on some leaves
which I scraped together and covered with my
jacket, and devoutly thanking God for saving
me from the horror of loosing myself and starv-
ing in the wilderness, and for all his kindness
thus far, composed myself to rest.

CHAPTER V.

Spencer is pursued and overtaken by the Indians—
Incidents on their return—Torture of his confinement
at night—Suffers from want of rest and food—Becomes
the property of Wawpawwawquaw—Arrive at an Indian village—Kindness shown him by a squaw.

THE sun had set, with promise of a fair morrow ; evening, mild and calm, had followed him ;
the soft twilight, gradually deepening, was fast
merging into night ; the birds had chanted their
vesper hymn, and a deep and universal stillness
reigned.   I felt that I was alone, in the midst
of a vast wilderness, exposed to prowling wolves
and deadly panthers, and my heart for a moment
sunk within me, from a sense of my utter help-
lessness, and of my inability to oppose even the
barrier of a fire between me and destruction ;
then the thought of home, and the hope of reaching it in safety, banished my fears, and inspired
me with fresh courage.   I had lain thus but a few
minutes, now closing my eyes to sleep, and now
opening them upon the spreading tree tops, or
stars faintly glimmering through their branches,
when I was suddenly roused by the cracking of
bushes, and a noise like that from quick strokes
on the ground, and looking toward the path,
saw a herd of deer bounding through the woods,
and swiftly approaching me.   Presently one of
them sprang over the log under which I lay ;
the others, leaping between me and the thicket,
where I had tied the horse, were in the next
moment out of sight.   Scarcely had I lain down

again, when, hearing a rustling among the bushes at a short distance from me, I raised myself upon my elbow to ascertain the cause; but words cannot express my feelings, nor describe my consternation and dismay, when, looking through an opening between the roots of the fallen tree under which I was lying, I saw the two Indians, whom I had left, enter the thicket. Advancing immediately to the horse, and laying hold of his bridle, they stood a few moments, looking in different directions through the small opening in the thicket facing my retreat, evidently endeavouring to discover me. I had by this time partially recovered my self possession, and fearing that if I waited for them to find me, they would tomahawk me where I lay, determined at once to return to them. Instantly springing up and putting on my jacket, I ran to the thicket, and with the mingled fear of deserved punishment, and the slight hope of impunity, uttered the truly childlike excuse, " I have been out picking raspberries."

Methinks I can now see the horrible savage grinding his teeth with rage, and with a look of fiendish malice, that almost froze my blood, raise his rifle to his shoulder, intending to shoot me. Were my mother's prayers now ascending before the throne? Was my father now supplicating protection for his lost son? Or had the Father of mercies said, " Lay not thine hand upon the lad?" At that moment the generous Wawpawwawquaw interposed, and throwing up the muzzle of the nearly leveled rifle, saved my

SPENCER NARROWLY ESCAPES BEING SHOT.

Page 59.

life. A brief altercation, and then a few moments'
earnest conversation ensued, after which, setting
down their rifles, and cutting large switches from
the thicket, they beat me severely on my head
and shoulders, until their whips were literally
"used up." I bore their beating, however,
with the firmness of an Indian; never once
complaining, nor entreating remission, but not
daring to make farther resistance than to throw
up my arms to protect my head. Often since
have I felt thankful, that there were none other
than sassafras bushes near; for had the Indians
thus beaten me with hickory or oak, they would
certainly have killed me. Having wearied
themselves in punishing me, and having told me
by signs, which I could not misunderstand, that
if again I should attempt to escape, they would
certainly kill and scalp me, we set out for our
camp, the White Loon in front, leading me by
the hand, and the other Indian following on the
horse, until we reached the path, when we proceeded along it in single file.

If at any time I flagged a little, falling too far
behind the leading Indian, the cruel savage behind me goaded me with a stick, or strove to
ride over me; and after proceeding about two
miles, discovering in the path the bark hopples I
had thrown down, he sprung from the horse,
and picking them up, inflicted many severe
blows with them on my head and shoulders.—
Weary and faint, I rejoiced, when at last we
reached the camp; but my satisfaction was
momentary only, for without stopping even to

secure the horse, the Indians proceeded to tie
me. Passing a cord around my elbows, they
drew them together behind my back so closely,
as to almost dislocate my shoulders ; then tying
my wrists so tightly, as nearly to prevent the circulation of the blood in my hands, they fastened
the ends of the cord to a forked stake driven into
the ground. I had often, as I thought, suffered not a little, but my sufferings this night were
extreme ; I could not lie down, and to sleep was
impossible ; my head, bruised and swollen, pained
me exceedingly, but this was trivial when compared with the torture I suffered, from the violent
straining of my arms behind my back ; my ribs
seemed every moment as though they would be
torn from my breast, and my shoulder blades
felt as if they would separate from my body.—
Forgetting the late signal instances of Divine in-
terposition, I murmured against God, and in the
bitterness of my soul longed for death.

The night seemed as if it would never end ;
but at length the day dawned, and gratefully
did I hail the cheerful sunrise, when the Indians,
having eaten their breakfast, and being ready to
march, came and unbinding me, relieved me
from the severity of suffering. Immediately fording Buck creek (the eastern branch of Mad River)
here about thirty feet wide, and swelled by the
late rain, rising above my waist, we passed on in
a north-westerly direction, through the eastern
side of a prairie, near to a high woodland, about
a mile and a half, and crossing Mad River (an
important branch of the Great Miami) at a broad

SPENCER TIED FOR THE NIGHT.

Page 63.

ford, sixty feet wide, ascended a high bank, matted with blue grass, covered with raspberry bushes, and plum trees, and exhibiting the appearance of having been once the site of an Indian village. Here the Indians stopping a few minutes to adjust their blankets, and make a pair of bark stirrups, I availed myself of the opportunity to breakfast on the raspberries, which were very abundant. Travelling on in a north-west course, through open woods, over high rolling ground, about noon we descended into a rich bottom, and halted on the bank of a small creek near a fine spring. Distant from this spot a few rods was a very large sycamore, hollow at the bottom, and having on the side facing us an opening, about six feet high, barricaded below with logs, covered with brush. To this tree the Indians immediately proceeded, and removing the brush from before it, and looking into its hollow for a moment, returned to the spring, where making a fire and roasting some squirrels which they had killed in the morning, made their dinner.— I had eaten nothing but raspberries for the last twenty-four hours; I was very hungry; yet the Indians offered me no food. I thought of their late cruel treatment to me, and of their continued inhumanity. I looked at the opening of the hollow sycamore, which appeared black within, as if it had been burned, and suddenly was seized with the apprehension that they there intended to burn me. Weak and faint from want of rest, of food, and from the debilitating effects of a severe dysentery with which I had been seized in the

5

morning; stiff and sore from beating and from confinement, my feet swelled from walking, and my legs torn with briers, I was truly an object of pity. I sat with my back toward the Indians, ruminating on my wretched condition and gloomy prospects, now begging for death to release me from my sufferings, and now shrinking from the thought of its pains, its terrors, and above all, from that eternity beyond it, for which I felt that I was wholly unprepared. Soon, however, I found relief in a flood of tears, which I carefully concealed from the Indians, and washing my face, and bathing my throbbing temples at the brook, strove to assume the semblance of cheerfulness. The Indians now leading the horse out to the hollow sycamore, and removing the logs from before its opening, I soon discovered the cause of their late haste to examine it, and with that discovery dismissed my foolish apprehensions. It is worthy of remark, that in their villages the Indians use neither bolts nor locks, and that when they leave for a time their cabins, either empty or with any articles in them, a log placed against its door affords ample protection to its contents, and abundant evidence of the right of possession in its owner; a right, seldom, if ever violated, even by the most worthless among them. The same respect is paid, even in the wilderness, to property, known or believed to belong to Indians of the same tribe, or to those of other tribes at peace with them.

If discovered, their property here had remained inviolate; and now taking from within the hollow tree an old blanket and packsaddle, and fastening them upon the horse's back, the Indians next brought out two large packs of deer skins of equal size, neatly folded, and firmly tied together, and connecting them with tugs of raw hide, and placing them on the saddle so that they hung about half way down his sides, made them fast with a cord; then securing between the packs a small brass kettle, made to contain about two gallons, and completing the contents of the tree, we took up our line of march. Providing me with a switch, and placing me next to the horse, Wawpawwawquaw followed, ordering me to urge him forward, and whenever he lagged, touching me with his wiping stick, and pointing to the lazy animal, would cry, "Howh caucheeh," meaning, that I should quicken his gait. This employment gave me a little excitement, and helped to rouse me from a lethargy produced by sickness and weariness; but from which nothing could have effectually quickened me, save the certain expectation of death, the moment that from any cause I should be unable to proceed. From the conduct of the Indians, I suspected, what I afterward found to be the fact, that after my late attempt to escape from them, I became the property of Wawpawwawquaw, by purchase from the other Indian, who now exercised no control over me. This gave me some comfort, as my former master, (a Shawnee,) beside being an ugly looking fellow, and having something sinister in his countenance, evidenced a very cruel and savage disposition, and withal great meanness and selfishness; and indeed, to me, seemed destitute of every manly feeling; while Wawpawwawquaw, (the son of a Mohawk chief, now, from the almost utter extinction of his nation, united with the Shawnees,) though in battle fierce as brave, was at other times (for a savage) humane and benevolent. His person, a little above the middle size, was well formed, combining activity with strength; his face was fine; his countenance open and intelligent, and his bearing noble and manly. True, like all Indians, under deep wrongs, he was vindictive; but while some of his nation, deserting its ranks, fought on the side of its oppressors, disdaining to aid his natural enemies to crush the remnant of his race, he remained unchangeable in his opposition to the "pale faces," bravely resisting their continued aggressions, so long as there appeared to be the slightest hope of preventing their farther encroachment; then yielding to the power of circumstances, submitting calmly to his fate.

Having travelled since morning about thirty miles, two hours before sunset we forded a large stream, (then to me waist high,) to which Wawpawwawquaw pointing, said, Miami;' and which from its course here, a little north of west, from its long rapid, and from the appearance of the banks on both sides, I have since been satisfied that we crossed about two miles above Sidney. We encamped in the evening about six miles beyond the Miami, at a small creek; where, for the first time in thirty-six hours, making a hearty meal, I slept quietly through the night, and awoke in the morning greatly refreshed. In the course of a few hours' travelling this morning, crossing a great many small branches running in various directions, and then passing through a very extensive prairie, we came to a stream running northwardly, and following its course until noon, halted by the side of a small rivulet. Having no provisions, Wawpawwawquaw went to hunt some, but soon returned unsuccessful. Just at this time, a large hawk flying over our heads with a snake in his talons, and alighting on a tree a short distance from us, was brought down with the rifle, and being dressed by plucking out the larger, and singeing off the smaller feathers, and then boiled in our brass kettle with a quantity of milk weed, in about half an hour furnished us a dinner of flesh, soup, and greens. Even the Indians ate sparingly; for myself, though hungry, I found the hawk so tough and strong, that I could eat but a few mouthfuls; as for the soup and greens, without salt, the taste was not only insipid, but sickening. About the middle of the afternoon, we met a small company of Indian hunters, the first human beings we had seen since we left the Ohio. Here resting a while, after making, as I supposed, various inquiries about their own families, Wawpawwawquaw related all the particulars of their late expedition, describing, by the most significant gestures, their ambush, our approach, their firing, the fall of one man and the escape of the other by swimming, their taking me prisoner, and finally exhibiting the scalp, as a trophy of their exploit. This relation was heard by the hunters with profound attention, interrupted only at suitable times with proper expressions of wonder, or of praise; after which, purchasing of them, for a small silver brooch, a few pieces of dried venison, we resumed our journey, travelling near the bank of the same stream, (which I afterward found to be the Auglaize,) until sunset, then supping on boiled venison, lay down to rest.

Still travelling down the Auglaize, about three hours after sunrise on the morning of the 12th July, we came in sight of an Indian village; when Wawpawwawquaw cutting a long pole, tied the scalp to the end of it, and elevating it over his head, raised the scalp-halloo, a shrill whoop, which both Indians repeated frequently, until we entered the town. Here we found all its inhabitants assembled; more than fifty men, women, and children, collected in front of the nearest cabin, who, as soon as the first salutations by the principal men were ended, seating themselves, some on logs, and some on the ground, listened with deep attention, while Wawpawwawquaw, with that gravity of manner, and those intonations of voice, peculiar to Indian chiefs and warriors, again told the story of my captivity. He was proceeding at last to describe the act of tomahawking and scalping the unfortunate white man, when a little old Indian suddenly springing upon me, and throwing me down with violence, gave a loud shout, accompanied with many extravagant and furious gesticulations, and vociferating, (as I was afterward told,) that he had

vanquished his enemy. Immediately all the
women began to scream, and the children, down
to the small pappoose, setting up a long shrill
war whoop, gathered around me; I clung to
Wawpawwawquaw, but young as I was, I should
have been compelled to run the gauntlet through
the women and infant warriors, had I not from
great debility, occasioned by dysentery, been
scarcely able to move faster than a walk. About
noon that day we arrived at another village on
the Auglaize. Here also the inhabitants flocked
out to meet us, and in like manner were enter-
tained with an account of the late expedition of
the Indians, and the story of my captivity : but
although the women and children manifested a
great deal of curiosity, examining my dress, and
scanning me from head to feet, none of them
offered me any rudeness. An elderly, noble-
looking Indian, whom I took to be the village
chief, now led us to his cabin, where his wife,
who appeared to be a very mild and humane
woman, gave us first some boiled hommony, and
then a little corn cake and boiled venison. This
to me, at that time more than half starved, was a
most delicious repast. I ate very heartily, and
rising from my seat, and handing my kind hostess
the bowl out of which I had eaten, bowing low,
gratefully thanked her. She smiled, and only
said, *Enee, that is right, you are welcome,* or as if
wishing to lessen the sense of favour conferred,
It is nothing. From this village we travelled
leisurely on, occasionally passing an Indian hut,
and toward evening stopped at the cabin of Waw-

punnoo, a tall stout warrior, a brother of Wawpawwawquaw. His wife was quite a handsome
woman, delicately formed, and much fairer than
the generality of squaws; she seemed to possess
withal a very amiable disposition, and bore the
churlish treatment of her husband with a meek-
ness and patience that would adorn a Christian ;
although it was evident, she felt mortified that
others should witness his unkind conduct. By
the by, the Indians in general are not kind and
affectionate to their women, whom they treat
rather as slaves than as companions, compelling
them not only to perform the drudgery of the
household, but even to work in the field, it being
thought disgraceful for an Indian to labour.

I have often seen families travelling, and while
the poor squaw, bending under the weight of a
heavy load, and the girls carrying packs, or the
smaller children on their shoulders, were labouring along, the lazy Indian in front might be seen,
with nothing but his rifle and blanket, and the
boys with only a bow and arrows, or a reed blow
gun.

This night, for the first time since my captivity,
I slept under a shelter ; and lying on a deer skin,
with a blanket over me, rested comfortably. The
next morning we breakfasted early, and a little
before noon of the 13th July, after a journey of
nearly six days, and travelling about one hundred
and eighty miles, we arrived at the point, at the
confluence of the Auglaize and Maumee, or Miami of the lake. Here, disposing of their deer
skins to a British Indian trader, the Indians

crossed over the Miami to a small bark cabin
near its bank, and directly opposite to the point ;
and leaving me in charge of its occupant, an old
widow, the mother of Wawpawwawquaw, departed for their homes, a village on the river, about
one mile below.

———

CHAPTER VI.

Cooh-coo-cheeh cures Spencer's sores—Description
of her house—Spencer, through despair of making his
escape, begins to feel himself at home.

COOH-COO-CHEEH, the old squaw in whose
charge Wawpawwawquaw had left me, being in
that advanced stage of life in which we seek for
rest and quiet, apprehending no doubt, from my
squalid appearance and diseased state, an increase of her cares and labours, at first received
me with reluctance ; but surveying my emaciated
form, and examining my scratched and festered
limbs, my swelled feet, retaining when pressed
the print of the finger, and my toes, from the
friction of the sand collected in my moccasons
in frequently fording creeks, raw, and worn
almost to the bone, her pity was excited, some
of the dormant feelings of the mother were
awakened, and she soon began to apply herself
to my relief.   Having first effected at the river
a complete ablution of my person, she proceeded
to wash my clothes, in the meantime compelling
me to lie on a blanket for three or four hours
under the scorching sun, until my back was one

entire blister; then boiling a strong decoction of
red oak, and wild cherry bark, and dewberry
root, of which I drank frequently, and in which
I occasionally soaked my feet, for several days,
she effected in a short time a perfect cure. She
was a princess of the Wolf tribe of the Iroquois,
formerly living on the Sorel. Her person, about
the ordinary stature, was stout and clumsy; her
features were rather homely, and her expression, generally, harsh and repulsive, though at
times, when her thoughts were withdrawn from
the deep and weightier matters of futurity, or
when no longer conversing with the spirits of
other worlds, she felt that she was an inhabitant
of this, and resumed her interest in its concerns,
she was cheerful, and occasionally quite sociable, relating many pleasant stories and amusing
incidents of her early life. She was beside, a
sort of priestess, to whom the Indians applied
before going on any important war expedition,
inquiring whether they should be successful; and
from whom they generally received answers,
framed in such obscure and ambiguous terms,
as to confirm and increase her reputation, even
when an expedition proved most disastrous.—
Cooh-coo-cheeh was also esteemed a very great
medicine woman, eminently skilful in the pre-
paration of specifics believed to be of great effi-
cacy; but whose extraordinary virtues were
more particularly attributed to her powerful incantations, and her influence with the good spirits, with whom she professed to hold daily intercourse. Her husband had been a distinguished

war chief of the Mohawks, a nation formerly occupying the country along the St. Lawrence as far as Lake Ontario, and that bordering on lakes George and Champlain. This nation, toward the close of the 17th century, or about the year 1670, confederating with the Senecas, the Oneidas, the Cayugas, and the Onondagas, and forming what was then called the Five Nations (since, by the addition of the Tuscarawas expelled from North Carolina, called the Six Nations,) conquering most of the nations southward and west of them, claimed the territory as far west as the Mississippi, and southward to the Cherokee, or Tennessee River. Utterly destroying some nations, of whom not a vestige now remains; and incorporating others whom they had vanquished, they formed a powerful confederacy, and beside possessing superior bravery and consummate skill in war, they were formidable to the western tribes, in their wars with whom they were generally successful. The Mohawks were the early and firm allies of the British, and maintained their supremacy over the northern tribes, until about the year 1770, when, being totally defeated by the American colonists, they lost their ascendancy, yielded their claim of paramount authority, and, reduced and scattered, were in turn incorporated with other Indian nations, over whom they had once ruled.

After this signal defeat and loss of the Mohawks, the husband of Cooh-coo-cheeh, with his family, consisting of his wife, three sons, and a daughter, had removed from the St. Lawrence, and settled at the Shawnee village, a mile below the mouth of the Auglaize. In the victory of the Indians over a part of the army of Harmar, under Hardin and Willis, in October, 1790, in a furious charge made against the regulars, while in the act of tomahawking a soldier, he received a mortal wound from a bayonet, and dying on his way home, was buried on the bank of the Maumee, about twenty miles from the battle ground. Soon after his death his widow chose her residence, and erected her bark cabin on the spot now occupied by her; and having only a few months before, at the feast of the dead, with pious affection removed the remains of her late husband from their first resting place, interred them only a few rods above her dwelling, near to the war path, so that she might not only enjoy the happiness of conversing with him, but that his own spirit might be refreshed from viewing the warriors as they crossed the Maumee on their war expeditions, until having ended his probation, and being prepared for his journey, he should travel to the final abode of good spirits in the land far west, abounding with game, and enjoy all those sensual delights which, in the mind of an Indian, constitute heaven. Buried in a sitting posture, facing the west, by his side had been placed his rifle, tomahawk, knife, blanket, moccasons, and every thing necessary for a hunter and a warrior; and his friends had beside thrown many little articles, as presents, into his grave, at the head of which they placed a post about four feet high, painted red, and having near its top,

rudely carved, the image of a face; while below was marked the number of scalps he had
taken in battle, scalps of all colours, of hair of
all lengths, which, on some great occasions,
might be seen streaming in the wind, suspended
from a high pole bending over his grave, where
I once counted nineteen, torn from the heads of
my unfortunate countrymen.

The family of Cooh-coo-cheeh consisted of a
dark Indian girl (an orphan) two years my elder,
and a half Indian boy, about a year younger than
myself, both her grand children by her only
daughter, now the wife of George Ironside, a
British Indian trader, living at the trading station, on the high point directly opposite to her
cabin, a few hundred yards above the mouth of
Auglaize. The boy, reputed to be the son of
the famous, or rather infamous renegade, Simon
Girty, was very sprightly, but withal, passionate
and wilful, a perfectly spoiled child, to whom his
mother gave the Mohawk name of Ked-zaw-saw,
while his grandmother called him Simo-ne; the
girl, rather homely, but cheerful and good na-
tured, with bright, laughing eyes, was named
So-tone-goo; but called by the old squaw,
Qua-say.

To those who have never seen the dwelling
of an Indian priestess, a description of the bark
cabin of Cooh-coo-cheeh may perhaps be worth
the reading.

Covering an area of fourteen, by twenty-eight
feet, its frame was constructed of small poles, of
which some, planted upright in the ground, served

as posts and studs, supporting the ridge poles
and eve bearers, while others, firmly tied to these
by thongs of hickory bark, formed girders,
braces, laths, and rafters. This frame was
covered with large pieces of elm bark, seven or
eight feet long, and three or four feet wide;
which being pressed flat, and well dried to prevent their curling, fastened to the poles by thongs
of bark, formed the weather boarding, and roof
of the cabin. At its western end, was a narrow
doorway, about six feet high, closed, when necessary, by a single piece of bark placed beside
it, and fastened by a brace, set either within, or
on the outside, as occasion required. Within,
separated by a bark partition, were two apartments, of which the inner one, seldom entered
but by the old squaw, was occupied as a pantry,
a spare bed room, and at times as a sanctuary,
where she performed her incantations; the
other, having on each side a low frame covered
with bark and overspread with deer skins, serving both for seats and bedsteads, was in common
use by the family, both as a lodging, sitting,
cooking, and eating room. On the ground, in
the centre of this apartment, was placed the fire;
and over it, suspended from the ridge pole in
the middle of an aperture left for the passage of
the smoke, was a wooden trammel, for the convenience of cooking. The site of this cabin was
truly pleasant. It stood a few rods from the
northern bank of the Maumee, with its side fronting that river, on an elevated spot, from which
the ground first gently descending about one hun-

INDIAN PRIESTESS' HOUSE.

Page 79.

dred yards northward, thence gradually ascended
to the top of the table land bounding the narrow
bottom, extending about two miles above, and
the same distance below.

On the high ground was a beautiful open wood,
principally of oak and hickory ; while the bottom, with the exception of about five acres above
the cabin, cultivated with corn, and a small spot
around it, was covered with bushes, interspersed
with sapplings, and a few blue and white ash, and
elm trees. Both banks of the Maumee above the
Auglaize were steep and high ; that on which
our cabin stood was covered with willows, while
the opposite bank down to the point, being swept
by the current, here slightly curving, northeastwardly, as it mingled with the waters of its tri-
butary stream, was entirely bare. Immediately
below the point, the Auglaize running from the
southwest, and bending northeastwardly near its
mouth, washing the eastern side of the point,
entering obliquely and mingling its current with
the Maumee, occasioned in freshets a whirl and
boiling of the water in the centre, and strong
eddies on both sides of the river ; but in a low
stage, the water below the point, and for some
distance up each river, was perfectly still. The
Maumee, above the point, about one hundred
and twenty yards wide, and directly below it, a
hundred and seventy, is here, in its centre, in the
lowest stage of water, about seven feet deep ;
although its depth, where it has a current, is ordinarily not more than three. It abounds with
excellent fish, which the Indians generally take

6

with a gig, or shoot with arrows, and sometimes
with rifle balls ; but in this latter method of
taking them, requiring great judgment and a
practised eye, they are rarely successful, particularly where the water is deep, and very clear ;
the fish seeming to be within a few inches of
the surface, when he is at the same time so far
below it that the ball flattening, does not reach
him. On the south side of the Maumee, for
some distance below the mouth, and extending
more than a mile up the Auglaize, to an Indian
village, the low rich bottom, about three quarters of a mile in width, was one entire field,
covered with corn ; which being in tassel, presented a beautiful appearance. It is perhaps
not generally known, that formerly the Indian
women inhabiting large villages, wherever it was
practicable, cultivated portions of the same field,
separated from each other only by spaces of a few
feet, and varying in size according to the number and strength of their families ; seldom raising
corn as an article of commerce, but merely to
furnish bread for their own subsistence. Around
these large fields they made no inclosures ; nor
indeed, having no cattle, hogs, nor sheep, were
fences necessary.   As for their few horses, they
were either driven out into the woods, or secured
near their cabins, and having bells on, were easily prevented from trespassing, by the boys, whose
duty it was, by turns, while amusing themselves
with their bows and arrows, to protect the fields.

I had lived in my new habitation about a
week ; and having given up all hope of escaping,

which I now considered impossible, began to regard it as my future home. True, the home from which I had been torn, and the beloved parents from whom I feared that I was for ever separated, were seldom from my thoughts ; yet I strove to be cheerful, and by my ready obedience to ingratiate myself with Cooh-coo-cheeh, for whose kindness I felt grateful ; and who, with the blessing of Divine Providence, having restored me to health, took some pains to comfort and amuse me. Her son-in-law, a respectable Indian trader, supplied her occasionally with a few necessaries ; while from the Indians who consulted her on most important matters, she received presents of venison, and skins, and brooches, the common circulating medium among them. Her household furniture consisted of a large brass kettle, for washing and sugar making ; a deep, close-covered, copper hommony kettle ; a few knives, tin cups, pewter and horn spoons, sieves, wooden bowls, and baskets of various sizes ; a hommony block, and four beds and bedding, comprising each a few deer skins and two blankets ; so that, altogether, her circumstances were considered to be quite comfortable. Her dress, like that of the old squaws in general, was very plain and simple, consisting of a calico shirt, extending about six inches below the waist, and fastened at the bosom with a silver brooch ; a stroud or petticoat, simply a yard and a half of six quarter blue cloth with white selvidge, wrapped around her waist and confined with a girdle, and extending a little below the knee; a pair of leggins, or Indian stockings, of the same cloth, sewed so as to fit the leg, leaving a border of two inches, projecting from the outside and extending to the instep, and a pair of plain moccasons. The form of the dress is the same among the Indian women of all ranks and ages, varying only in its quality, and in the richness and variety with which it is adorned; its ornaments not being regulated by rank or station, but by the ability of the wearer. All the young and middle aged among the women are passionately fond of finery; the young belles, particularly, having the tops of their moccasons curiously wrought with beads, ribands, and porcupine quills; the borders of their leggins, and the bottoms and edges of their strouds tastily bound with ribands, edged with beads of various colours; and frequently on their moccasons and their leggins, small tufts of deer's hair, dyed red and confined in small pieces of tin, rattling as they walked, and forcibly reminding one of the "tinkling ornaments" worn by the Jewish women. Beside these ornaments, according to their ability, they covered the bosoms, shoulders, sides, and bottoms of their shirts (sometimes made of cross-barred silk handkerchiefs) with large and small silver brooches; and wore on their wrists and arms silver bracelets, from one to four inches in width. Nor is the fondness for show confined to the women; on the contrary, it is even stronger in the men, who, in addition to the ornaments worn by the women, wear large silver medals and gorgets on

the breast, silver rings in the nose, and heavy
pieces of silver in the ears ; the rims of which
being separated from the cartilage by cutting,
are weighed down two or three inches from the
head. A trifling circumstance, which I omitted
to mention, may illustrate their extreme love of
show. When captured, my roundabout and
pantaloons were of plain summer wear, with
covered mold buttons ; but my vest was of blue
silk, double-breasted, with two rows of small,
plated sugar-loaf buttons, which, attracting their
attention, the Indians had several times examined, supposing them to be silver. On the
second night after leaving the Ohio, the companion of Wawpawwawquaw, taking my vest, cut
off both rows of buttons, including a strip of two
inches of the silk on each side, and carefully fold-
ing them up, put them in his bullet pouch. Surprised at his conduct, and unable to form any
idea of his motive in spoiling my vest, I thought
he was actuated by a savage malignity merely,
and felt not a little chagrined and indignant,
when, just before entering the first Indian village,
I saw him fasten the spoils of my vest around
his legs, as garters, contrasting strangely with
his greasy leathern leggins.

It was now about the 21st of July, and being
a leisure time with Cooh-coo-cheeh, principally,
perhaps, to indulge her own inclination, and part-
ly to amuse me, she took me on a visit to the
Shawnee village, below us. We were kindly received by Wawpawwawquaw, whose wife, a very
pleasant, and rather pretty woman of twenty-five,

according to custom, set before us some refreshment, consisting of dried green corn boiled with beans and dried pumpkins, and making, as I thought, a very excellent dish.   After spending a few hours with this family, we went to pay our respects to the village chief, the celebrated Blue Jacket.   This chief was the most noble in appearance of any Indian I ever saw.   His person, about six feet high, was finely proportioned, stout and muscular ; his eyes large, bright, and piercing ; his forehead high and broad ; his nose aquiline ; his mouth rather wide, and his countenance open and intelligent, expressive of firmness and decision ; he was considered one of the most brave and accomplished of the Indian chiefs, second only to Little Turtle and Buck-on-ge-ha-la, having signalized himself on many occasions, particularly in the defeats of Colonel Hardin, and Gen. St. Clair.   He held (as I was told) the commission, and received the half pay of a brigadier general, from the British crown. On this day, receiving a visit from the Snake, chief of a neighbouring Shawnee village, and from Simon Girty, he was dressed in a scarlet frock coat, richly laced with gold, and confined around his waist with a party-coloured sash, and in red leggins and moccasons, ornamented in the highest style of Indian fashion.   On his shoulders he wore a pair of gold epauletts, and on his arms broad silver bracelets ; while from his neck hung a massive silver gorget, and a large medallion of his majesty George III.   Around his lodge were hung rifles, war clubs, bows and ar-

rows, and other implements of war ; while the
skins of deer, bear, panther, and otter, the spoils
of the chase, furnished pouches for tobacco, or
mats for seats and beds.   His wife was a remarkably fine-looking woman ; his daughters,
much fairer than the generality of Indian women, were quite handsome ; and his two sons,
about eighteen and twenty years old, educated
by the British, were very intelligent.   One of
the visiters of Blue Jacket, (the Snake,) was a
plain, grave chief, of sage appearance ; the
other, Simon Girty, whether it was from preju-
dice, associating with his look the fact, that he
was a renegado, the murderer of his own countrymen, racking his diabolic invention to inflict
new and more excruciating tortures, or not, his
dark shaggy hair ; his low forehead ; his brows
contracted, and meeting above his short flat
nose ; his grey sunken eyes, averting the inge-
nuous gaze ; his lips thin and compressed, and
the dark and sinister expression of his countenance, to me, seemed the very picture of a vil-
lain.   He wore the Indian costume, but without
any ornament ; and his silk handkerchief, while
it supplied the place of a hat, hid an unsightly
wound in his forehead.   On each side, in his
belt, was stuck a silver mounted pistol, and at his
left hung a short broad dirk, serving occasionally
the uses of a knife.   He made of me many inquiries ; some about my family, and the particulars
of my captivity ; but more of the strength of the
different garrisons ; the number of American
troops at Fort Washington, and whether the

president intended soon to send another army against the Indians. He spoke of the wrongs he had received at the hands of his countrymen, and with fiendish exultation of the revenge he had taken. He boasted of his exploits, of the number of his victories, and of his personal prowess; then raising his handkerchief, and exhibiting the deep wound in ꞏhis forehead, (which I was afterward told was inflicted by the tomahawk of the celebrated Indian chief, Brandt, in a drunken frolic,) said it was a sabre cut, which he received in battle at St. Clair's defeat; adding with an oath, that he had "sent the d——d Yankee officer" that gave it, "to h—l." He ended by telling me that I would never see home; but if I should "turn out to be a good hunter, and a brave warrior, I might one day be a chief." His presence and conversation having rendered my situation painful, I was not a little relieved when, a few hours after, ending our visit, we returned to our quiet lodge on the bank of the Maumee.

———

CHAPTER VII.

Spencer spends a day very pleasantly among the traders—Dines with Mr. Ironside, who treats him with great kindness—Sees William Moore—The feast of green corn—Indian games.

A few days after my visit to Blue Jacket's village, I accompanied Cooh-coo-cheeh over to the point, the residence of her daughter. On

this high ground, (since the site of Fort Defiance,
erected by General Wayne in 1794,) extending
from the Maumee a quarter of a mile up the
Auglaize, about two hundred yards in width,
was an open space, on the west and south of
which were oak woods, with hazel undergrowth.
Within this opening, a few hundred yards above
the point, on the steep high bank of the Auglaize,
were five or six cabins and log houses, inhabited
principally by Indian traders. The most northerly, a large hewed log house, divided below into
three apartments, was occupied as a warehouse,
store, and dwelling, by George Ironside, the most
wealthy and influential of the traders on the point.
Next to his were the houses of Pirault (Pero,) a
French baker, and M'Kenzie, a Scot, who, in
addition to merchandizing, followed the occupa-
tion of a silversmith, exchanging with the Indians
his brooches, ear-drops, and other silver ornaments at an enormous profit, for skins and furs.
Still farther up were several other families of
French and English ; and two American prisoners, Henry Ball, a soldier taken at St. Clair's
defeat, and his wife, Polly Meadows, captured at
the same time, were allowed to live here, and by
labour to pay their masters the price of their
ransom ; he by boating to the rapids of the
Maumee, and she by washing and sewing.—
Fronting the house of Ironside, and about fifty
yards from the bank, was a small stockade, en-
closing two hewed log houses ; one of which was
occupied by James Girty, (brother of Simon,)

the other, occasionally, by M'Kee and Elliot, British Indian agents, living at Detroit.

From this station I had a fine view of the large village more than a mile south, on the east side of the Auglaize, of Blue Jacket's town, and of the Maumee River for several miles below, and of the extensive prairie covered with corn, directly opposite, and forming together a very handsome landscape. I spent this day very pleasantly among the traders, dining with Mr. Ironside, who treated me with great kindness. I found him to be a very sociable and intelligent man; humane and benevolent. He seemed much interested in the story of my captivity, appeared to sympathize with me, gave me some useful advice and direction for the regulation of my conduct, and a great deal of information relative to the Indians, their history, customs, and manners. On the following day I was highly gratified in seeing at our cabin my late townsman, William Moore, who had just returned from a trip to the rapids, about sixty miles below. Moore was a stout, sinewy, muscular man, six feet two inches high; active, bold, and daring; combining the qualities and peculiarities of the western boatman and hunter; one, who in Kentucky would, in former years, have been termed "half horse, half alligator;" a practised marksman, who at fifty steps, with his rifle, "off hand," often "drove the centre," and seldom failed to "cut the black:" on the keel, pushing the first pole, and in running, jumping, wrestling, and other athletic exercises, having few superiors. Fear-

less and lawless, he was governed only by his
own sense of propriety and right; naturally good
humoured and obliging, but when roused, a perfect savage; and bold and powerful must have
been the man that would encounter and overcome
him. He had been taken prisoner by Wawpawwawquaw, his brother Caw-ta-waw-waw-
quaw, (Black Loon,) and three other Indians, a
few months preceding my captivity, about five
miles north of Columbia, on the waters of Mill
creek, where he had been hunting. He had just
killed a fine doe, and having lashed it on his
shoulders, had proceeded a few steps on his
return home, when the Indians, who had been
watching his movements, and waiting until he
should be encumbered with his load, fired upon
him from his right. One of their balls grazed
his right shoulder blade, another passing through
the carpus, or compact bones of the wrist, rendered powerless his left hand. Springing forward
on the instant, for the first hundred yards, even
with his load, he outran the Indians; meanwhile,
placing his rifle on his left shoulder, and throwing
his wounded hand over it, with his right cutting
the lashings, disencumbered himself of his burden,
and in a few minutes distanced all but two of his
pursuers. Gaining the top of a ridge, and looking back upon the first Indians, the foremost of
whom was several rods behind him, he gave a
loud whoop, and deridingly slapping his thigh,
bounded off like a deer to the foot of the hill.
Here, failing in the attempt to leap a creek, his
feet slipped on the edge of the opposite bank,

and he fell backward into the water. By the time he had risen to his feet and recovered his rifle, which had fallen into the water, he was overtaken by Wawpawwawquaw, who, leaping down the bank, twice snapped his pistol at him. Moore, meantime levelling his rifle, also twice attempted to shoot the Indian; but unfortunately its priming was wet, and he had no opportunity to renew it. Clubbing his gun, he next attempted to strike down his adversary, but his left hand being powerless, his stroke was easily parried. He now threw down his rifle, and drawing his knife, was just about to close in deadly strife, when the brother of Wawpawwawquaw that moment reaching the spot, interfered. Becoming faint from loss of blood, seeing the remaining Indians close at hand, and considering farther resistance, or attempt to escape, useless, Moore picked up his rifle, and surrendered it to Waw-pawwawquaw, who, extending to him his hand, received him as his prisoner.

On his arrival at Blue Jacket's village, Moore being only a private prisoner to one whose family had then no manes to appease, or blood to retribute, was not subjected to the disposal of a council; but custom immemorial requiring, that as a man and a warrior, he should run the gauntlet, an early day was fixed for the interesting exhibition. That day soon arrived; and men, women, and children, invited from the neighbouring villages, flocked to the capital of the Shawnees, anticipating as much pleasure as we would expect at the celebration of our nation's anniversary.

Here, after gratifying their curiosity in examining the prisoner, armed with clubs, switches, and
other instruments of punishment, they arranged
themselves facing each other, in two rows, about
seven feet apart, and numbering more than two
hundred persons, each distant four or five feet
from each other, extending three hundred yards
along the level space between the village and
the Maumee River. The chiefs and principal
warriors stood at the head of the lines, within a
few rods of the cabin selected as the goal, while
the rest of the men, with the women and the
youths, promiscuously occupied the other parts.
Moore was now led out and stripped to the waist,
when the Indians, aware of his strength and
activity, tied together his wrists, for the double
purpose of hindering his speed and of preventing
him from retaliating on his tormentors, yet so as
to afford him the means of protecting his face.
Starting a short distance from the head of the
lines, he soon bounded through them ; and
breathing a few moments, returning with the
same speed, had reached the middle of his
course, when the Indians, fearing that from his
fleetness he would run through with little injury,
(as most of their blows, instead of falling on his
back, fell clattering on each others' sticks,) half
closing their ranks, attempted to obstruct his
progress. Appealing in vain to their sense of
honour and justice, frequently crying, (as he told
me,) " Honour bright," and " fair play," and
finding that he would probably be severely
beaten, he undertook, himself, to redress his

wrongs; and so effectually did he use his feet, head, and right fist, kicking some, striking down others, and with his head overturning a number, that the rest readily made way, and opening for him an ample passage, amidst the shouts of the warriors, he soon reached the goal. Having passed the ordinary trial, he was now congratulated as a brave man, and by some applauded for his late resistance; all but the sufferers being highly diverted at his successful expedient to rid himself of a severe beating.

Moore was a great favourite of Cooh-coo-cheeh, to whose comfort and accommodation he had largely contributed. But a short time before my arrival, he had added to her solitary room an additional cabin, and now, preparatory to the feast of green corn, he was engaged in erecting for her a bark shed, closed at the back, and facing our cabin, a few rods distant on the west, and elevated about three feet from the ground, for the accommodation of her more aged guests, who, unable to take any active part in them, might here witness the exercises and sports of the day. It was on a pleasant morning, about the middle of August, when the ears of corn, grown to full size, were yet in that soft milky state in which they are used for roasting, that the three sons of Cooh-coo-cheeh, with their wives; her daughter, with her husband, Mr. Ironside; Capt. Walker, and some other Shawnee warriors, with their wives, and a few old squaws, in compliance with her invitation, assembled at our cabin to celebrate the feast of *green corn.* This is a festival said to be similar to that of "*first fruits*" among the Jews (and by some, used as an argument to prove that the aborigines of America were descendants of that nation;) when the more wealthy and influential among the Indians of the same tribe, ostensibly, to evidence their gratitude to the Great Spirit for his manifold mercies, inviting the members and relatives of their respective families, feast them principally on green corn, variously cooked, and entertain them with different games and sports; usually crowning their festivities with copious draughts of " fire water" —either rum or whiskey.

Here, after the usual salutations at meeting, when all were assembled and seated on the grass, and the pipe, according to custom, had several times passed round the circle, a venerable Indian arose, and with much solemnity of tone and earnestness of manner, addressed them. He spoke (as Mr. Ironside afterward informed me) of the distinguishing favour of the Great Spirit to his red children, the first and most honourable of the human race, to whom he had given the vast country stretching from the sun's rising place, in the far east, to where it sets in the great waters beyond the Rocky Mountains; extending from the frozen sea of the north, to the boundless salt waters of the south; yielding abundantly, corn for bread, supplying meat and clothing for their families, from the buffalo, the elk, the deer, and every variety of wild game with which the forest once abounded; producing spontaneously the most valuable medicinal plants, furnishing specifics for every disease to which his red children were exposed; of their obligations to him for all these benefits, especially for sending them fruitful showers, and now blessing them with an earnest of a good crop of corn, and that they ought to evidence their sense of obligation to him, by gratefully feasting on his bounties there provided for them, and by heartily engaging in the manly sports and exercises of the day. He then spoke of the "pale faces," whom he represented as the first murderers and oppressors; ascribed their own sad reverses to the anger of the Great Spirit, for affording these murderers an asylum on their shores; of their duty to exterminate, if possible, these intruders on their soil, at least to drive them south of the Ohio. He said that their late victories over the whites, particularly their signal defeat of St. Clair, were evidences of the returning favour of the Great Spirit; and concluded by exhorting them to deeds of valour, and to conquest of their natural enemies, as a certain passport to the boundless hunting grounds in the far, "far west," beyond the vast waters, where the Great Spirit would never suffer the "pale faces" to enter. This speech was listened to by all with deep attention; the auditors improving each brief pause to utter some monosyllable expressive of the various feelings that by turns inspired them; but at the concluding sentence, as if actuated by one sentiment, simultaneously springing to their feet and uttering a shrill and prolonged whoop, with grea·

animation they commenced their sports. The first of these was running on foot over a straight course of about one hundred yards, in which the principal competitors were the White and Black Loons, Wawpunnoo, and Captain Walker ; Moore not being allowed, at the beginning, to join in their sports. And here, for the first time, having an opportunity of witnessing the fleetness of the Indians, I noticed that in running (as in walking) they turned their toes in, hindering the full force of the muscles of the leg ; and that their movements resembled more the bounding of the deer than the more rapid steps of the whites, whose lower, forward efforts, bore them only onward. And I am satisfied, that although from habit, continuing to breathe freely, the Indians may run longer at great speed, yet, in a short race, they are generally less fleet than the whites. Wawpawwawquaw, whose movements were lower and more rapid, won the race ; though Moore swore that he could give him twenty steps and beat him in a hundred yards.

In the wrestling that followed, Wawpunnoo (brother of the Loons) and Capt. Walker, both tall and powerful men, bore off the palm ; but in repeated trials with each other, with various success, Walker was acknowledged victor. Wawwawwawquaw, however, having been several times severely thrown by Walker, now insisted that he should wrestle with Moore. To this Walker objected, intimating that it would be rather a stoop to wrestle with a prisoner ; but the Loon insisting, and at the same time leading

7

Moore forward, he reluctantly advanced to meet him. Their first essays, as is usual with practised wrestlers, were but partial trials of each other's strength and skill; but at length exerting their powers, the contest was long and apparently doubtful; each by turns being raised from his feet, seemed about to be thrown with violence by his antagonist, or bent to the ground by his powerful arms, when Moore, availing himself of an unguarded movement of his adversary, with a trip of his foot and a sudden twist of his body, threw him to the ground, yet partially with his arms sustaining him while falling, so that he suffered no injury. Mortified at his failure, and more than half angry, Walker sprung to his feet, and again closing with Moore, and straining every muscle of his body, put forth all his strength. The struggle, however, was short; for Moore, being now excited, losing sight of his former prudence, by a powerful effort raising his antagonist on his hip, pitched him heels over head, stretching with violence his whole length upon the ground. This occasioned a loud *waugh!* from the other Indians, and no small gratification to the White Loon; but Moore, perceiving that he had roused the resentment of Walker, and excited the jealousy of the rest, strove to allay their feelings, and by magnifying the strength of his antagonist, and ascribing his own success rather to accident than to superior power and skill, soon succeeded in restoring good humour. It being now about noon, the Indians suspended their sports to partake of the plentiful feast provided by Cooh-coo-cheeh, consisting of boiled jerk and fish, stewed squirrels and venison, and green corn boiled, some in the ear, and some cut from the cob and mixed with beans, beside squashes and roasted pumpkins. For bread, beside that prepared in the ordinary way from corn meal, we had some made of the green corn, cut from the cob and pounded in a mortar until it was brought to the consistency of thick cream, then being salted and poured into a sort of mold of an oblong form, more than half the length and twice the thickness of a man's hand, made of corn leaves, and baked in the ashes, was very palatable. The guests did ample justice to the entertainment, eating very heartily out of the wooden bowls in which their dinner was served, and which they held in their laps, using their own knives to cut their meat, which they held in their fingers, and the horn, wooden, and pewter spoons of their hostess, in eating their succotash; each man and woman as they finished their dinner, setting down their bowl saying, "Ooway nelah, netape hooloo;" literally, I have done, my stomach is full. Having all dined, and enjoyed for a few minutes the (with them) great luxury of smoking, a small keg of rum was produced, to the great gratification of the guests, all of whom, both men and women, took a hearty draught; when the men, giving their knives and tomahawks in charge to Cooh-coo-cheeh, arose to renew their sports.

CHAPTER VIII.

Indians excessively fond of strong drink—Revenge-
ful when intoxicated—A farther account of Indian
games—Spencer becomes expert with his bow and
arrow—Meets with Wells, then a prisoner at large
among the Indians, who becomes interested for him
and gives information to the commander at Post Vincennes, which soon reaches his father—Measures are
adopted to obtain his liberty—A body of warriors consult Cooh-coo-cheeh about the success of their expedition against the whites—Spencer in full Indian costume—Narrow escape from a wild cat.

The Indians are extravagantly fond of spirit-
uous liquor; not only the men, but the women,
when they can obtain it, drinking to excess.—
Aware, however, of its mischievous consequences,
they always, before deliberately commencing a
drunken revel, select some one to remain sober,
to whose charge they commit their knives, tomahawks, and other dangerous weapons, and whose
duty it is carefully to secrete and retain these
until after their carousal, when they shall have
become perfectly sober; so that very rarely at
their revels, more serious injuries occur than
bruised eyes or bloody noses. And when at
their drinking bouts, brawls take place, and
blows and wounds succeed, the injuries they
suffer are entirely overlooked when sober; all
their acts committed in a state of ebriety being
ascribed wholly to the "fire water." On their
way home (usually at night) from their carousals,
they always give notice of their coming—singing,
or rather roaring, their drunken song, "Ha yaw

ki-you-wan-nie, Hi haw nit-ta-koo-pee," the
notes of which, rather plaintive and dirge-like,
are more varied than their generally monotonous tunes; and sung quicker or slower,
louder or less vociferously, not only indicate the
age and temper, but mark with great certainty
the degree of intoxication of the individual; one,
very drunk, prolonging each note, sometimes
sounding as if the singer had made a sudden
lurch to one side, or a stagger on the other. If
the Indian be one whom drunkenness renders
more savage and brutal, his wife, or any mem-
ber of his family with whom he may have been
offended when sober, now has a warning, which
is seldom neglected, to keep out of his way; as
he not unfrequently avails himself of the cover
of ebriety to revenge, with impunity, some injury he had received when sober. At such
times, and under such circumstances, it is pecu-
liarly dangerous for prisoners (many of whom
fall a sacrifice to the brutal barbarity of drunken
Indians,) to encounter them. Once when in
company with White Loon and Moore, who
were shooting fish, near Blue Jacket's village, I
saw from the canoe the body of a youth of fourteen, (who, with his sister, a girl of sixteen, had
been taken prisoners by the Indians from some
settlement on the Ohio, a short time after my
captivity,) who had been tomahawked and scalped, and mangled in the most brutal manner by
his drunken master, who, not taking the trouble
even to bury him, left him to rot near the edge
of the Maumee. I myself have often been

obliged in the middle of winter, when the ground
was covered with a deep snow, at the well-
known, dreaded sounds of "ki-you-wan-nie," to
spring from my bed, and seizing only a blanket,
run and hide behind the nearest log or tree, or
throw myself down in the snow, where I have
laid for more than an hour, not daring to move
until the drunkard had gone off; and once I
narrowly escaped death.   I had, unfortunately,
offended Black Loon, who, some nights afterward, returning home drunk, from the Miami
village, a few miles west of us, came so near to
our cabin before I was aware of his approach,
that I had scarcely time to escape.   Entering
the door, he inquired for me, and being told that
I was absent, struck his knife several times
through the skins on my bunk; then seizing a
cat which lay near him, threw it on the fire, and
placing his foot upon it, kept it there, (the poor
animal squalling most piteously the while,) until
Cooh-coo-cheeh jerking it out, threw it into the
snow.   This poor Indian, fighting in our cause
in the late war with Great Britain, was unfortunately killed near Manary's block house, a few
miles from Bellefontaine, by one of our rangers,
supposing him to be a spy of the enemy.   At the
close of the last chapter I left the Indians, who
had just dined, about to resume their festive
games; and as it may possibly interest some of
my readers, I will briefly describe one or two
more, ending the sports of the feast of green corn.

The men now formed a circle, within, and
near the edge of which, one of the strongest,

lying on his back, held firmly in his hands between his raised knees, a piece of raw hide,
made soft by soaking, and so slippery from
greasing, as to require a powerful grasp, and a
strong hand to wrest it from his gripe.   Following each other at the distance of about three
feet, and moving several times around the circle
in quick time, with elastic step, sinking alternately on each foot, and singing, " A yaw wha-
no heigh, how-wa-yow-wa," in one of their most
monotonous tunes, each Indian in succession
giving a loud " whoop-haw," suddenly stooped,
and firmly grasping the raw hide, strove to draw
it from the hands of its holder.   Failing in this,
or drawing it suddenly from his hands, some not
unfrequently measured their length upon the
ground, to the no small amusement of the others ;
but the wresting it from the hands of the holder,
or raising him by it from the ground erect upon
his feet, was held to be a proof of superior
strength.   Dancing now began ; the men moving
in an outer, and the women in an inner circle,
stepping lightly, and rather gracefully sinking
with a rocking motion, first on one foot, then on
the other ; or changing the form, facing each
other in lines, sometimes springing up briskly,
with a sort of galloping motion, at others, with
their bodies bent forward, slowly raising both feet
at once and bringing them down heavily, uttering a " heigh" at every jump, while an old man
pounding with one stick upon a small drum, sung
at the same time, slowly or more lively, according to the kind of dance, regulating the steps of

the dancers, who kept exact time with the music.
It was now the middle of the afternoon, and
both men and women, with the exception of
Cooh-coo-cheeh, were more than half drunk.—
Moore had prudently retired with Mr. Ironside
across the Maumee, and I had withdrawn to the
corn fields; where, however, looking through a
small hole in the back of the shed, I could, without danger, witness the movements of the Indians.
They now drank more frequently; some dancing
singly, others in groups; some singing, some
whooping, and some quarrelling, until at length,
"uproar wild and deep confusion reigned."—
About this time Wawpawwawquaw, smarting
probably under the recollection of the severe
falls he had received from Walker, laying hold of
him and insisting on another trial of his skill in
wrestling, was unfortunately thrown into the fire
and severely burned. This disaster served as a
signal for bringing the festivities to a close;
and in a very short time all the guests, staggering off in different directions, departed for their
respective homes.

Little worth relating occurred for nearly two
months. In the meantime, having nothing to
do except to bring water, and collect wood for
cooking, I had some leisure, which I occupied
in hunting with a bow and arrow, in the use of
which I became quite expert, frequently shooting birds, and at one time killing a fine rabbit,
which I bore to the cabin with no small degree
of pride, and to the great satisfaction of the old
squaw, to whom it furnished a delicious repast,

and of Sotonegoo, who congratulated me, telling
me that I would soon become a man and a hunter. Sometimes, too, I was permitted to visit the
Trader's Station, on the point, where I was always welcomed by Mr. Ironside, and treated
with great kindness by his wife, the daughter of
Cooh-coo-cheeh. It was on one of these visits,
in the woods above the point, as I before related,
that I saw Wells, then a prisoner at large among
the Indians, who, having learned my name, inquired very particularly about my family, their
residence and rank. The information which I
gave him he soon communicated to the officer
commanding at Post Vincennes, by whom it

was sent to Col. Wilkinson at Fort Washington, and by him immediately to my father. Through the influence of Gen. Washington, letters were obtained from the British minister at Philadelphia, to Col. Simcoe, governor of Upper Canada, which were conveyed to him by an express, despatched by my friends through the state of New-York to Niagara; so that while abandoning all hope of seeing again my home and my beloved kindred, I was striving to become reconciled to my fate, active preparations were making for my release, and measures were in operation, which, under the blessing of Providence, in a few months afterward, resulted in my deliverance. About the middle of October, the Indians learning through their spies, that either an expedition against some of their towns was contemplated by the Americans, or that provisions were on the way to supply the outposts under a strong convoy, soon assembled a force of two hundred warriors, (Shawnees and Miamies,) under the celebrated Little Turtle, and marched to attack them. On their way to join the Miamies, who had encamped near the point, the two Loons and about fifty Shawnee warriors from Snake's town and Blue Jacket's village, halted near our cabin, and sent to consult Cooh-coo-cheeh about the success of their expedition. The old woman immediately entered her sanctuary, where she remained nearly an hour, during a part of which time, sitting under the shed, I could hear the noise as of a stick striking the sides of the cabin, and the beds, and particularly the kettles within it; and afterward a low humming sound of the voice, at which time I supposed she was uttering her incantations. Coming out soon after with a countenance unusually animated, though with a look of great wildness, she stretched out both arms, and then gradually bringing the tips of her fingers together, as if encircling something, exclaimed, "Mechee! mechee! mechee!" which the Indians, instantly interpreting to be, many sclaps, many prisoners, and much plunder, reported to the party, who, fired with the confident expectation of success, immediately proceeded to join the main body. I had never before seen so large a force of Indian warriors, and while I could not but admire their fine forms and warlike appearance, as they marched in single file to the river, or stood erect in their canoes, with their rifles in their hands, crossing the Maumee, I shuddered at the thought of the lives that would be taken, and the hundreds that through their instrumentality would soon be made widows, orphans, and childless. Young as I then was, I could not help at times looking on the old woman with a superstitious fear, mingled with awe. I did not believe that she was divinely inspired, but thought it more than probable that she held intercourse with evil spirits; nor was that fear and awe lessened when, about the middle of November, the Indians, under Little Turtle, returned victorious, having defeated a body of troops, principally Kentuckians, (or Semonthe, as they termed them,) near Fort St. Clair, taking several scalps, a large number of horses,

and a great deal of baggage. Wawpawwawquaw and his brother had each a good horse
and a number of new blankets; and some of the
Indians packed home tents, camp kettles, and
many other articles. The Shawnees gave
Cooh-coo-cheeh six blankets and several pounds
of tobacco, beside a small keg of whiskey, (part
of their spoils,) in gratitude for the aid which
they doubted not she had afforded them in
achieving their victory; while their late success, if possible, increased their confidence in
her supposed supernatural power. The weather had now become cold, and my summer
clothes, being not only too thin for the season,
but nearly worn out, were thrown aside; and a
white shirt, blanket capot, blue leggins, and waist
cloth, supplied their place, so that I was dressed
in full Indian costume.

Although the labour of gathering their corn
was over, I found pretty constant employment;
I had now to make fires, carry water both
for cooking and drinking, wash the hommony
when boiled in ashes, and assist the old woman
in getting wood. One afternoon in December,
Cooh-coo-cheeh being engaged, sent me alone to
cut and bring home an armful of wood. Taking
the axe, the pecawn, (a long strap for tying up
the wood,) and our faithful dog, who generally
accompanied me, I went about a quarter of a
mile up the bottom; where, having cut some
wood and tied it into a bundle, I was just about
to place it on my back, when the dog, moving
off cautiously a few rods, sat down near a small

tree, where, growling fiercely and striking the
ground with his tail, he first looked up toward the
top of a sappling, and then at me, as if to inform me
there was game there, and to ask my assistance.
Picking up the axe, I walked deliberately to the
dog, and following the direction of his eyes, saw
on a limb about sixteen feet from the ground, an
animal of a dark gray colour mixed with red,
with a white belly and round head, altogether
resembling a cat, but four times larger than the
largest tame cat, and couched like that animal
when ready to spring upon its prey. Ignorant
of its nature, and unapprehensive of danger, I
threw several sticks at it to induce it to come

down ; at length, hitting it severely on the head,
it sprang to the ground within a few feet of me,
when the dog instantly seizing it, a fierce contest
ensued.   The dog being strong, active, and cou-
rageous, several times caught the animal by the
throat, but was as often compelled to let go his
hold, so fiercely and powerfully did his antagonist, drawing up his hind feet, apply his sharp
claws to his breast and sides.   Indeed, I now
began to fear he would conquer the dog, whose
ardour seemed to have considerably abated, and
who fought with greater caution : approaching
with the axe, and taking advantage of an opportunity when the dog again attempted to seize
the throat of the animal, I was so fortunate as to
hit him a severe blow on the head, completely
stunning him ; then left him to his enraged antagonist, who soon finished the work of death.—
The dog, though severely wounded, appeared to
be delighted ; now standing over his fallen enemy as if exulting in his death, and now jumping
around me, wagging his tail with pleasure.   For
myself, I turned the animal over several times ;
marked his length, which, from his nose to the
end of his tail, I judged to be about four feet ;
then examining him particularly, for the first
time suspected that he was either a wild cat or
a young panther.   Leaving my wood, and
shouldering my prize, I marched home, and with
no small exultation threw my load down before
Cooh-coo-cheeh, who, raising her hands with
surprise, exclaimed, " Waugh haugh—h ! Poo-
shun !"   It proved, indeed, to be a large male

wild cat ; an animal equally insidious and dangerous, according to its size and strength, as a
panther ; and which, but for the presence of the
dog, and my own ignorance of its nature, and
of my danger, might have destroyed me.   This
exploit, with which the old woman associated
great courage and daring, raised me very much
in her estimation.   She heard all the particulars
of the affair with great satisfaction, and frequently saying, " Enee, wessah," (that is right,
that is good,) said I would one day become a
great hunter, and placing her fore fingers together, (by which sign the Indians represent marriage,) and then pointing to Sotonegoo, told me
that when I should become a man I should have
her for a wife.   I had now acquired a sufficient
knowledge of the Shawnee tongue to understand
all ordinary conversation, and indeed the greater
part of all that I heard ; (accompanied, as their
conversation and speeches were, with the most
significant gestures ;) and often in the long winter evenings listened with much pleasure, and
sometimes with deep interest, to Cooh-coo-cheeh,
as she told of the bloody battles of her nation,
particularly with the Americans ; of the great
prowess of her ancestors ; their chivalrous exploits and " deeds of noble daring," or related
some interesting events of her early life ; her
courtship and marriage ; the great strength,
bravery, and activity of her then young husband,
Co-kun-di-aw-thah, and her own youthful
charms.   Her memory seemed a great store-
house, out of which she brought " things new

and old." In almost all her tales, however,
whether tragic or mirthful, whether of great
achievements in the battle and in the chase, or
whether relating some diverting incident or humorous story, she mingled many superstitious
ideas, and spoke much of supernatural agency,
and of her own frequent intercourse and conversation with departed spirits. To the beaver she
not only gave the faculty of reason, but the
power of speech; and I shall ever recollect the
song, said by her to have been sung by a beaver
to an almost desponding hunter, stayed by a
freshet and half starved; encouragingly telling
him that the high waters would soon subside,
and that beyond the stream he should find plenty
of game.

> " Sawwattee sawwatty,
>   Sawwattee sawwatty,
>   Sawawkee meechee noo kahoohonny;
>   Kooquay nippee ta tsa;
>   Waugh waw waugh whaw,
>   Waugh waw waugh whaw."

Cooh-coo-cheeh took much pains to learn me
to dance; an accomplishment not so easily acquired as, from the great simplicity of their steps,
might at first be supposed; grace, with them,
consisting principally in the motions of the body;
the action of their limbs being rather adapted to
facilitate and perfect these, (and not, as with us,
at least in former days, the chief exhibiters of
grace and skill,) and it required much practice
to combine both successfully. Having seen my
elder instruct my younger sister in dancing, I

had learned several steps, particularly the ba-
lancer, and single and double chasser, and sometimes for the amusement of Cooh-coo-cheeh I
gave her a specimen of the manner of our dancing : with the slower and more simple steps
she seemed to be amused, occasionally laughing
heartily at what to her appeared so ludicrous ;
but when I attempted a hornpipe, whirling round
frequently, or capered along in a double chasser,
so ridiculous did it appear to her, manifesting, as
she thought, such a want of grace and dignity,
that usually, with some marked expression of
contempt, she put a stop to my farther exhibition.
Cooh-coo-cheeh was remarkably nice in her
cookery ; requiring her kettles to be scoured
often, and her bowls and spoons to be washed
daily, and nothing offended her quicker than the
appearance of sluttishness ; and although I stood
pretty high in her favour, I sometimes incurred
her displeasure by my neglect, particularly by my
want of cleanliness, as she thought, in performing some of my household duties. On a very
cold morning, about the middle of January, she
had risen before day, and intending to make
some hommony, had boiled the corn for some
time with ashes to remove its hulls. It was my
duty to cleanse it from the ashes, and as it had
been long enough in them, I was ordered to get
up and perform that duty. The old woman's
temper was very quick, and when roused, she
was like a fury ; and by no means particular in
selecting an instrument of punishment, when her
poker was not at hand, seized a knife, axe, billet

8

of wood, any thing within her reach, hurling it at the unfortunate subject of her wrath. Not rising immediately, she uttered her customary Oogh! followed by a stroke of her poker, and not giving me time to put on my moccasons, hurried me off with the kettle of boiling corn and a large coarse sieve to the river. The Maumee had for some time been frozen over, and through the ice, about six inches thick, we had cut and kept open a hole for the convenience of getting water. Placing the large sieve by the side of the opening, and emptying the corn into it, I proceeded to dip up water, pouring it on the hommony, which I rubbed well to take off the hulls. I had not finished my work when my bare feet, all this time standing on the ice, were so pained with cold that I could endure it no longer, and stepping into the hommony, was enjoying the luxury of its warmth when the old woman espied me.— Calling me loudly by my Indian name, Mecheeway, and uttering several ooghs, she ran down furious with rage to the river, and hurling her poker, inflicted a severe blow on my back, felling me to the ice. Immediately, however, springing up, I ran off, leaving her to finish the hommony, and did not return to the cabin until her anger had subsided.

CHAPTER IX.

Sugar making—British Indian agent arrives to release Spencer—Affection of Cooh-coo-cheeh at parting —Arrives at Detroit on March 3d.

It was now near the close of February, when sharp, frosty nights, and days of warm sunshine, succeeding the extreme cold of winter, constituted what in early times in the west was called *sugar weather ;* a season always improved by most families, who drew their year's supply from the sugar tree ; and some made, beside, quantities of sugar for sale. Taking our large brass kettle, with several smaller ones, some corn and beans for our sustenance, our bedding, and indeed all our household furniture and utensils, excepting the hommony block, we closed our cabin door, placing the customary stick against it, crossed the Maumee below the mouth of the Auglaize, and packing our baggage on a horse, proceeded four or five miles down the river to a beautiful open woods, principally of sugar trees, intermixed with blue ash, elm, and poplar. Here Cooh-coo-cheeh had for many years made her sugar, and here we found a comfortable bark shelter, with every convenience for sugar making, save kettles, which we now supplied. I here found constant employment : dusting out and setting the troughs, as the old woman tapped the trees ; carrying the sap, cutting wood, making fires, and occasionally attending to boiling the water at night. We had had a remarkably fine season, and had been for several days employed, during which time we had collected sap sufficient to make, probably, a hundred weight of sugar, when one evening near sunset, as we were quietly seated around the fire, a messenger came and privately informed Cooh-coo-cheeh, that the British Indian agent from Detroit had arrived at Auglaize, and having purchased me of Mr. Ironside, (who had been authorized by Wawpawwawquaw, now absent on a hunting expedition, to dispose of me,) he had been sent to conduct me to the Point. Whether it was that she thought that the sudden joy which the news of my release from captivity would inspire, might prove injurious to me; or whether she herself, having now become rather attached to me, was unwilling to part with me, the old woman received the intelligence, (which she did not communicate to me until the next morning,) with great seriousness, answering only with a simple Hu! enee.

That evening she seemed more than usually disposed to converse with me, and repeating her inquiries about my parents, their rank in society, how long they had lived on the Ohio, and many such questions, asked me particularly of the place of their former residence; and when I told her that they once lived not far from the sea shore, and near New-York; and that their forefathers were English, who came from the island on the eastern side of the great salt lake, south and east of us, her brow for a moment seemed deeply clouded, and the mournful tones of her voice betrayed her mingled feeling of melancholy and

regret. She spoke of the first landing of the
"pale faces" from their monstrous canoes, with
their great white wings, as seen by her ancestors; of their early settlements, their rapid
growth, their widely-spreading population, their
increasing strength and power, their insatiable
avarice, and their continued encroachments on
the red men; who, reduced by diseases, thinned
by civil wars, and diminished by their long and
various struggles, first with the British, (Met-
a-coo-se-a-qua,) then with Se-mon-the, (the
Americans or Long-knives,) were no longer
powerful; and that they would not be satisfied
until they had crowded the Indians to the extreme
north, to perish on the great Ice lake; or to the
far west, until pushing those who should escape
from their rifles, into the great waters, all would
at length be exterminated. She spoke of the
anger of the Great Spirit against the red men,
especially those of her own nation, nearly all of
whom had perished; and that herself and her
children, the remnant of her race, would soon
sleep in the ground, and that there would be none
to gather them at the feast of the dead, or to
celebrate their obsequies. But her countenance
soon kindled with animation, and her eyes spar-
kled with pleasure, when changing the mournful
theme, she ended with a most glowing description
of the beautiful hunting grounds, the ever-during
abode of the brave and good red men. These she
described as lying far, far beyond the vast western
ocean, and as being ten-fold larger than the great
continent of America. There, she said, the

changing seasons brought no extremes of heat
or cold, wet or drought; none were sick, none
became old or infirm; and well do I recollect,
that pointing to the large poplars near us, some
of which were five or six feet in diameter, and
rose eighty feet without a limb, she spoke of the
largest trees of that country as being twenty
times larger, and spreading their broad tops
among the stars.   Corn, and beans, and pumpkins, and melons, she said, grew there spontaneously; the trees were loaded with the richest
fruits; the ground was clothed with perpetual
verdure, and the flowers on the prairies were
ever blooming and fragrant; the springs were
abundant, clear and cool; the rivers large, deep,
and transparent, abounding with fish of endless
varieties; the fine open woods were stocked
with innumerable herds of buffalos, deer, elk,
and moose, and every species of game: in short,
there was a paradise containing all that could
delight the mind or gratify the senses, and to
crown all, the exclusive home of the Indian.—
The little Canadian Frenchman, for such was
the messenger, listened with that attention, which,
among the Indians, is inseparable from good
manners; frequently expressing his admiration
and even his wonder, though once or twice
turning to me and smiling incredulously, he said,
" Ma foi ! dat is grand contry."

We arose early the next morning, when the
Frenchman expressing his intention to set out
immediately for the Point, Cooh-coo-chech, now
for the first time communicating to me the infor-

mation he had given her on the preceding night,
told me that I should go down to Detroit, cross
the great lake in a big canoe, and performing a
large circuit, arrive at my home on the Ohio.—
She spoke of the happiness of my family, especially the joy of my mother at my safe return;
then of her own regret in parting with me, having, as she said, began to regard me as her child;
and concluded by saying, that if I should grow
up to be a man, I must come and see her. She
was affected even to tears, as taking my hands
in both of hers and cordially pressing them, she
bade me adieu. Poor Sotonegoo sobbed loudly
as I took her hand, and for the moment deeply
affected, bade her farewell.

I now, leaving the cabin, followed the Frenchman at a brisk pace; frequently, however, looking back at its inmates, who were still standing
near it, until the intervening trees hid them for
ever from my sight. It was a very pleasant
morning, on the last day of February, 1793, that
I bade adieu to my Indian friends. The sun,
just rising, seemed to shine with unusual splen-
dour; never before, as I thought, had he appeared so bright and beautiful. I had been at
first "as one that dreamed," scarcely crediting
the fact that I was no longer a prisoner; gradually, however, as I left my late dwelling farther
and farther behind me, becoming assured and
conscious of the truth that I was *indeed free*, I
was like a bird loosed from his cage, or a young
colt from his stall; to suppress my feelings, or
restrain my joy would have been almost impossi-

ble. I laughed, I wept, I whistled, I shouted,
and sung by turns; never had I moved with
step so elastic; now skipping over logs, jumping, dancing, and running alternately, while the
Frenchman (whose name I found on inquiry to
be Joseph Blanche) sometimes stopped and
looked at me intently as if suspecting that I was
more than half insane. By degrees, however,
this extreme of joy subsiding, I became more
temperate, confining the expression of my happiness to singing and whistling, which I kept
up almost without intermission until we reached
the Auglaize, when stepping into a canoe, and
crossing that river, in a few minutes we entered
the hospitable dwelling of Mr. Ironside. This
gentleman received me with more than his usual
kindness, and congratulating me heartily on my
release from Indian captivity, introduced me to
Col. Elliot, the British Indian agent, and to a
Mr. Sharp, a merchant of Detroit, who had accompanied him to Auglaize. Elliot received
me with considerable hauteur, and with a look
that spoke that his noticing me was condescension; and although, as I afterward learned, he
had been sent by the express order of Gov.
Simcoe to effect my ransom and convey me to
Detroit; yet, as if such a service was degrading,
he pretended, that being at Auglaize on public
business, he had accidentally heard of me, and
actuated wholly by motives of humanity, procured my release, for which he had agreed to
pay one hundred and twenty dollars. Having
understood from Cooh-coo-cheeh, that I was to

be sent home to my parents, I was not a little disappointed in finding, as I supposed, that I was the property of an individual and subject to be disposed of at his pleasure; however, I soon comforted myself with the thought, that the same humanity which had moved him to effect my ransom, would influence him to perfect the generous act by restoring me to my friends, and that at the worst, my condition would be greatly meliorated. Elliot, I have no doubt, had conveyed to Mr. Ironside the same false impression, that my ransom was altogether his own private affair; as that gentleman, equally scorning such pitiful deceit, to magnify his generosity, as incapable of trifling with the feelings of one in my hapless situation, would, had he known the truth, have immediately undeceived me. The wife of Ironside now kindly invited me to breakfast; but Elliot, objecting to the trouble it would give her, ordered Joseph to take me over to James Girty's, where he said our breakfast would be provided. Girty's wife soon furnished us with some coffee, wheat bread, and stewed pork and venison, of which (it being so much better than the food to which I had been lately accustomed) I ate with great *gout*; but I had not more than half breakfasted when Girty came in, and seating himself opposite to me, said, "So, my young Yankee, you're about to start for home." I answered, "Yes sir, I hope so." That, he said, would depend on my master, in whose kitchen he had no doubt I should first serve a few years apprenticeship as a scullion. Then taking his knife, said, (while sharpening it on a whetstone,) "I see your ears are whole yet, but I'm d—n—y mistaken if you leave this without the Indian ear mark, that we may know you when we catch you again." I did not wait to prove whether he was in jest, or in downright earnest; but leaving my breakfast half finished, I instantly sprang from the table, leaped out of the door, and in a few seconds took refuge in Mr. Ironside's house. On learning the cause of my flight, Elliot uttered a sardonic laugh, deriding my unfounded childish fears, as he was pleased to term them; but Ironside looked serious, shaking his head, as if he had no doubt that if I had remained, Girty would have executed his threat.

Every thing being now ready for our departure, we took our leave of Mr. Ironside and his wife (I with feelings of gratitude for their kindness, which I have never forgotten) and of several of the inhabitants on the Point, who wished us a good voyage, and me a safe return home; and seating ourselves in a small open bateau, steered by Joseph, and rowed by a stout Canadian whom he called Baptiste, we soon cleared the point, and began to descend the Maumee. Passing the cabin of Cooh-coocheeh, on its northern bank, I took a last look at the spot where I had spent more than seven months of hopeless captivity, and very many hours of painful solicitude and fearful apprehension. Nearly eight months before, I had arrived there, weary, exhausted, half famished, sick, desponding, and a prisoner, truly an object of pity ; now, although ragged, dirty, bareheaded, and very much tanned, my looks were by no means inviting, still I enjoyed good health ; and what with me seemed then to comprise almost every blessing, I was free from savage captivity. Turning my back for ever upon my late residence, with tears of gratitude I devoutly thanked God for my deliverance ; and as I thought that the ever-rolling current, aided by every stroke of the oar, was wafting me nearer and nearer home, I felt a pleasure which it would be impossible for me to describe. Of Elliot and Sharp I have but an indistinct recollection : they were both men of only ordinary size, having nothing remarkable in their appearance. Elliot's hair was black, his complexion dark, his features small ; his nose I recollect was short, turning up at the end, his look was haughty, and his countenance repulsive ; Sharp, on the contrary, had light hair and fair complexion, with a smirking look, and a countenance indicative of shallowness. After half an hour spent in light and unimportant conversation, Sharp, I suppose merely to pass away the time, requested me to relate the particulars of my captivity, with which, however, he appeared but little interested ; often interrupting me to make some observations on persons or things as we passed down the river. He then made several inquiries about my family, the Miami settlements, and Fort Washington ; which leading to a general conversation, drew from Elliot many ungentlemanly remarks, and disparaging observations about the Americans. Sharp then observed, that being so full of notions of liberty and equality, they would make rather stubborn servants, and that he thought I would be no great bargain ; however, he continued looking at me, " I suppose you will not have much employ-ment for him ?"   " Not much," replied Elliot, " beside cleaning knives and forks, blacking shoes, running of errands, and waiting upon table."   With an expression of disgust and in-dignation I turned my back upon him.   The truth was, I more than half doubted his having more to do with me that to convey me to Detroit. I asked no more questions of either of them, and when questioned, answered as briefly as possible ; amusing myself with looking at the nu-merous fish swimming in the clear stream, or at the lofty trees, with here and there an Indian hut, or village on its banks ; and now listening to the cheerful song of the boatmen as the one plied his oar and the other his paddle, timeing their strokes as exactly with their music as a soldier would the tread of his left foot with the flam of the drum.   On the first night after leaving the Au-glaize, we slept at a Wyandot village, and on the following morning passing the rapids, we landed about the middle of the afternoon on the northern bank of the Maumee, a few miles above its entrance into lake Erie, at a small encamp-ment of Wyandots.   Here the two boatmen, with their bateau, leaving us, proceeded to their home at Frenchtown ; and here Elliot placing me in charge of the Wyandots, with whom he had contracted probably for a gallon of rum, to convey me to Detroit, mounting his horse in company with Sharp, rode off, leaving me again to the mercy of the savages. The Indians, eight or ten in number, commenced drinking pretty freely, directly after Elliot left us, and soon becoming half drunk, began to sing, and dance, and shout, and wrestle, as usual. Among them was a youth of about fourteen, who, while I was sitting quietly as a spectator on one side of the tent, came, and pulling me up, insisted that I should wrestle with him. This I refused, objecting to the great inequality of our years, and size, and strength; but being urged, I at length consented ; and as I was very strong for one of my years, and withal quite active, in a very few seconds I laid him sprawling on the ground.— In a second effort he was more successful, throwing me down ; but the moment I struck the ground, giving a sudden spring, I threw myself over him, and as he struggled by force to get up, held him down, until he asked me to let him rise. Mortified and angry, he now got up, and seizing me by the hair, and passing his finger around my head, at the same time blackguarding me in broken Shawnee, said he would scalp me. That moment I gave him a severe blow in the pit of the stomach which, while it made him loose his hold upon my hair, nearly knocked him down. I now stood in an attitude of defence, determined to resent or resist any farther insult or violence : he did not now approach me ; but waiting an opportunity, when, supposing his anger had cooled, I had turned round and walked a few

steps with the intention of sitting down, drew
his knife, and stealing behind me, stabbed me in
the back. He no doubt intended to inflict a
mortal wound, but the knife fortunately striking
the lower part of my shoulder blade, glanced
down across the ribs, without entering the body ;
making an incision about an inch wide, and found
when afterward probed by the British surgeon at
Detroit to be three inches deep. An old Indian
now interfered, and discovering from the blood
that flowed, that I was badly wounded, stripped
off my capot, and pressing the wound firmly,
applied a large quid of tobacco to its orifice ;
then covering it with a compress, secured by a
bandage over my shoulder and round my chest,
effectually staunched the blood. Early next
morning (so great had been Elliot's care about
me) I was *confided to the charge of two old
squaws,* who placing me in the middle of their
canoe set out for Detroit (about forty-five miles
distant) and paddling along the edge of the lake
and up the strait, arriving at that place on the
evening of the third of March, delivered me to
Colonel Richard England, the officer commanding that garrison.

CHAPTER X.

Spencer is received with great kindness at Detroit
by Col. England and others—Sails for Fort Niagara—
Incidents on the passage.

COLONEL ENGLAND had been instructed by
Gov. Simcoe to receive me, to provide clothing,

and every thing necessary for my comfort, and
to send me on to Fort Niagara, as soon as the
navigation of Lake Erie should open. He had
beside been informed about my family, and particularly my relatives ; and was personally acquainted with some connections of my mother;
so that from his sense of duty, as well as from
a disposition to oblige his friends, I would have
been assured of a favourable reception. But,
independently of these considerations, being both
a gentleman and a man of great humanity, he
received me with much kindness ; and regard-
ing my wretched appearance, with sympathy
for my condition, followed only the generous
impulse of his nature, in ministering to my relief and comfort. After asking me some brief
questions, and kindly assuring me of my future
welfare, addressing himself to Lieut. Andre, an
officer of the same regiment, (who also expecting
me, had, on hearing of my arrival, repaired to the
colonel's quarters,) said, he committed me to
his charge, observing that Mr. Andre would of
course take pleasure in making the necessary
provision for me. Mr. Andre immediately took
me by the hand, and led me to his quarters in
the same barracks, only a few doors distant, and
requesting me to sit down, retired from the apartment. In a few minutes a servant entered, and
set before me some tea, and bread, and butter,
on which having supped, I arose, and was re-
tiring from the table, when two women, whom
mere curiosity, as I supposed, had kept standing
at one end of the room, looking at me intently

while I was eating, now advanced, and each, unceremoniously taking me by the hand, and leading me out of the apartment, conducted me to a chamber. Here, stripping off all but my shirt, carefully throwing my clothes out at a back window, beyond the palisades of the town, and seating me in a large washtub, half filled with water, they tore off my shirt, which had fast adhered to the bandage round my shoulder, before I had time to tell them I was wounded, and so suddenly, inflicting for a moment acute pain, as to extort from me a loud scream.—Their surprise at this soon ceased, when I told them that an Indian had stabbed me in the shoulder ; and when they saw the blood from the opened wound running down my back, one of them, alarmed, ran to inform Mr. Andre ; the other, with a rag immediately staunching the blood, deliberately proceeded to scour my person with soap and water, and by the time the surgeon arrived had effected a complete ablution. On probing the wound, which he found to be about three inches deep, the surgeon pronounced it to be not dangerous ; fortunately, he said, the knife, in entering, had struck the lower, posterior point of the right shoulder blade, and taken a direction downward ; but had it entered either an inch lower, or nearer the spine, it would probably have caused death. From the want of clothes, it was late next morning before I could get up ; but receiving at length a temporary supply of a roundabout and pantaloons, from the wardrobe of Ensign O'Brian, (brother of Mrs. England,) and a pair of stockings and slippers, from one of the women, I made my appearance in the breakfast room, and was introduced to Mrs. Andre, wife of the lieutenant.— She very kindly took my hand, and congratulated me on my deliverance from the Indians; though she could not help smiling at my singular appearance, dressed, as I was, in clothes which, although they fitted the smallest officer in the garrison, hung like bags on me. Mrs. Andre made very particular inquiries about my mother, (whose maiden name was Ogden,) and my relatives on her side; and telling me that she had been a Miss Ogden, made our relationship to be that of third cousins. This unexpected information gave me great pleasure; for to find among strangers, and in highly-polished society, one who was not ashamed to acknowledge, as a relative, a destitute boy, far from friends and home, could not but be truly gratifying. But Mrs. Andre possessed none of the false pride of those who, governed wholly by factitious circumstances, while they "have respect to the man in gay clothing," feeling as if degraded by condescension to the unfortunate, "say to the poor, Stand thou there." She was kind and amiable, as she was handsome and accomplished; and although quite young, apparently not more than twenty, supplied to me the place of a mother. Her husband, a brother of the unfortunate Major Andre, and one of the handsomest men I ever saw, very affable in his manners, and frank in his disposition, treated me with great kindness;

and after seeing that I was comfortably, and indeed genteelly dressed, introduced me to the families of Mr. Erskine and Commodore Grant, (where I found boys and girls of nearly my own age, who cheerfully associated with me,) and took pleasure in showing me the town, the shipping, the fort, and whatever else he thought would afford me gratification. Here, too, I frequently saw Moore, who, through the influence of Col. M'Kee, a countryman, and an old friend of his father, had obtained his liberty, and given him employment in the agency. He seemed quite contented, and even happy; amusing himself, in his leisure hours, in shooting at a mark; or in running, wrestling, jumping, or other athletic exercises.

The situation of Detroit, on the western bank of the strait, connecting Lake Huron with Lake Erie, and about ten miles south of Lake St. Clair, is familiar to all; though but few here have any knowledge of what it was more than forty years since. It was then a small town, containing only wooden buildings, but few of which were well finished; surrounded by high pickets, inclosing an area of probably half a mile square, about one third part of which, along the bank of the river, (as the strait is called,) was covered with houses. There were, I think, three narrow streets, running parallel with the river, and intersected by four or five more at right angles. At the south end of the town, adjoining on the west the second street, at the ends of which were the entrances, (secured by heavy wooden gates,) into the city,

was a space about two hundred feet square, inclosed on a part of two sides with low palisades,
within which a row of handsome three story barracks, for the accommodation of the officers, occupied the south side, and buildings of the same
height for the soldiers' quarters, stood on the
west, and a part of the north side. The open
space was occupied as a parade ground, where
the troops were every day exercised by the adjutant. In the northwest corner of the large area,
inclosed with pickets, on ground a little elevated,
stood the fort, separated from the houses by an
esplanade, and surrounded, first by an abatis
of tree tops, having the butts of the limbs sharp-
ened and projecting outward about four feet
high ; then by a deep ditch, in the centre of which
were high pickets ; and then by a row of light
palisades, seven or eight feet long, projecting ho-
rizontally from the glacis. The fort, covering not
more than half an acre of ground, was square,
having a bastion at each angle, with parapets
and ramparts, so high as to shelter the quarters
within, which were bomb proof, entirely from
the shot of an enemy. Its entrance was on the
east side, facing the river, over a drawbridge,
and through a covered way ; over which, on each
side, were long iron cannon, carrying twenty-
four pound shot, and which the officers called,
the " British lions ;" while on each of the other
sides were planted two, and on each bastion,
four cannon, of various calibre ; six, nine, and
twelve pounders. The fort was garrisoned by a
company of artillery, under the command of

Capt. Spear; while two companies of infantry, and one of grenadiers, of the 24th, (Col. England's regiment,) were quartered in the barracks; the balance of the regiment was at Michilimakinak, and other northern posts. By the side of the gate, near the end of the officers' barracks, was a twenty-four pounder; and for the protection of the east side of the town, there were two small batteries of cannon, on the bank of the river. In the spring of 1793, there were anchored in the river, in front of the town, three brigs of about two hundred tons each; the Chippewa and the Ottowa, new vessels, carrying each, I think, eight guns; the Dunmore, an old vessel of six guns, and a sloop, the Felicity, of about one hundred tons, armed only with two swivels; all belonging to his majesty, George III., and commanded by Com. Grant. There were beside, several merchantmen, sloops, and schooners, the property of individuals.

I had spent almost four weeks very agreeably at Detroit, becoming much attached to Col. England, and particularly so to Mr. and Mrs. Andre, who treated me with great kindness, and to the family of Mr. Erskine, who were very friendly and polite to me; and when, near the close of March, the lake being entirely clear of ice; and when, though there was some danger to be apprehended from easterly storms, it was thought that the navigation to Fort Erie would be tolerably safe, orders were issued for the sailing of the Felicity. I felt a momentary regret that I was so soon to be separated from these kind friends and acquaintances. Every thing being in readiness, and the sloop beginning to weigh anchor, I took leave of Mr. and Mrs. Andre, thanking them with tears for their parental kindness ; and so affected was I, that I could scarcely pronounce the word farewell. Of Col. England, also, who wished me a prosperous voyage, and safe return to my friends, I took a very affecting leave, acknowledging with gratitude my obligations to him ; then, with a small bundle containing a few shirts and stockings, accompanying the sailor who was waiting to conduct me, proceeded to the sloop's boat, and in a few minutes more was safe on board the Felicity.

With a light breeze we proceeded down the strait ; but the wind being from the southwest, we went but little faster than the current, as we were obliged to tack very frequently, from side to side of the river. Anchoring at its mouth, we lay there during the night ; and the next morning, the wind freshening a little from the same direction, we were enabled, in addition to our lower sails, to spread our topsail and top gallant sail, and about the middle of the afternoon anchored in Put-in-bay, a fine harbour in the western part of Lake Erie, formed by the North, Middle, and South Bass, the Strentian, and some smaller islands. The wind being light and variable, and there being some appearance of a change of weather, Capt. Fleming thought it most prudent to remain here until morning ; and taking me into the boat, with two oarsmen and a couple of hooks and lines, rowed round the

bay, trailing the lines from the stern. Passing along the north side of Strentian Island,
which is convex, steep and rocky, we caught
several fine bass, (one of which I had the pleasure of drawing into the boat,) on which we
made a delicious meal. On a high rocky point
of this island stood a very large tall tree, tower-
ing above the adjacent woods, on the top of
which was an eyry. Here first I saw the noble
American eagle, and amused myself for some
time watching several of them, as, without the
least apparent exertion, they gracefully, yet with
amazing velocity, compassed the bay; gradually
rising, and contracting their sphere with each
circuit, until, suddenly mounting, they seemed a
mere speck in the blue sky; then as suddenly
descending, almost with the rapidity of thought,
to mid air, they began to wheel around, doubling
their sphere with each circuit as they descended,
some lighting on the trees, others darting on
their prey. One of them lighted on the high
tree, near the nest, where his mate could be seen,
probably hatching her eggs, and whose place he
took soon after, as she left her nest for food or
recreation. Early next morning, it being the
first day of April, having a light breeze from the
south, we weighed anchor, and sailing eastward-
ly, in a few hours passed between Point Pelee
and Middle Islands; and at four o'clock in the
afternoon, (our sloop being a pretty good sailer,)
had made about fifty miles, when the wind suddenly coming round, began to blow fresh from
the east. We continued onward, however, re-

gularly tacking from southeast to northeast, as near to the wind as the vessel would progress, until after sunset; the wind still increasing. We were now out of sight of land; the water all around us seeming to touch the horizon, and the curling waves crested with foam, appearing to mingle with the clouds, presented to me a novel, sublime, and yet fearful spectacle. I had retired to my berth on the larboard side of the cabin, about ten o'clock, and notwithstanding the noise of the waves, and the pitching of the vessel, had fallen into a sound sleep, when the wind, having increased to a tempest, to proceed was impossible. For some time we lay to, under a close-reefed jib and main sail, when the captain, seeing no prospect of the storm's abating, and fearing that the rolling of the sloop would unship her mast, gave orders to put her about. In coming round on the starboard we were nearly upset. I was awakened by being thrown from my berth against the opposite side of the cabin; and the next moment a heavy sea striking the stern, and forcing in the cabin windows, poured in several hogsheads of water, in which, tossed about from side to side, it was nearly a minute before I could gain my feet, and ascend to the deck. The dead lights were, however, soon closed, and the vessel cleared of water, and I was advised by the captain to return to my berth in the cabin; but I preferred remaining on deck, thinking that if the sloop should be wrecked, I should have a much better chance of escape.— Although scudding almost under bare poles, (merely carrying sail enough to steer the vessel by,) we were going at the rate of twelve knots an hour, and pitching and rolling with the heavy swells, sometimes fearing that we should lose our mast, or that the seams of the vessel (rather old and unseaworthy) opening, she would founder ; or, the lake being shallow, that she would be dashed to pieces against the bottom. Providence, however, kindly preserved us, and just after daylight, passing the fearful breakers on the north side of Point Pelee, soon anchored safely in Put-in-bay. Tom, the cook, who was held as an oracle on board the sloop, openly declared that our being driven back by the storm, was in consequence of our sailing from the bay on Friday, being, beside, the first day of April, to which all the crew assented, adding that we were lucky in getting safely back. We spent a part of Saturday afternoon in an excursion through the Middle Bass Island, on which we killed several large rattlesnakes. I narrowly escaped being bitten by one, at least three feet long, over whom I stepped, as he crossed the path ; and the captain, who had gone to a small pond a few hundred yards ahead of us, to shoot ducks, returned in a short time, running, and out of breath, declaring that at the moment he fired at some ducks, a monster, a snake, more than a rod in length, issued from the long grass by the edge of the water, made directly toward him, and pursued him for more than twenty rods.— On our return to the sloop we caught some fine bass, which more than compensated us for the loss of the captain's ducks. The next morning, being Sunday, having the wind fresh from the south, and the weather being favourable, we again weighed anchor and stood out of the bay ; Tom prognosticating that we should have a prosperous voyage. His predictions seemed likely to be verified, as we sailed finely this day ; Tom entertaining us with several marvellous stories and extraordinary adventures, of which he had a store, and of which many would compare with those of " Sinbad the Sailor ;" beside, he had a great variety of nautical songs, some of which, as " Sweet Poll of Plymouth," and " All in the Downs," he sung with considerable pathos ; and others, of bloody battles, and brilliant victories, with great spirit ; but none of my entreaties could prevail with him to sing " Cease rude Boreas," which he said was to be sung only on shore, over a good can of grog, in company with wives and sweethearts. The wind, which had been favourable all Sunday, veered round before Monday morning, blowing very fresh directly ahead ; and soon after daylight, when in sight of Long or Puttshawk's Point, and not much more than a hundred miles from Fort Erie, to our great disappointment, a storm, even more furious than the first, compelled us to put about, and drove us quite back to Put-in-bay, which we reached on Monday evening. On Wednesday morning we again sailed, and on the day following were again driven back by a furious storm, which carried away our top gallant mast. On returning this time I was extremely sick from the pitching and rolling of the sloop, and began to be discouraged, fearing we should never get across the lake. We had in the hold of the sloop an ill-looking man, said to be an American, whom the British had taken up at Detroit, on suspicion of his being a spy ; and on whose person some papers, said to be plans of the fort and town, were found. Pronouncing him guilty, Col. England had ordered him to be heavily ironed, and put on board the sloop to be conveyed to Niagara. Tom now declared that this man was a Jonah ; on whose account the vessel had not been permitted to cross the lake. One, who though he had escaped justice on shore, the Almighty would not suffer to reach the land alive ; and so deeply were the crew imbued with this sentiment, that but for a discovery made on the following day, they might have been tempted to execute their threats, which they had privately made, to throw him overboard. On Friday morning, the wind being still fresh from the east, the captain proposed that we should go a fishing, and then make a little excursion through the North Bass Island. Making a compass round westerly, and northerly, in our boat ; catching a few fine bass, a small sturgeon, and some white fish, we proceeded to the middle of the south side of the North Bass Island, and crossing it in a north-easterly direction to its north shore, were attracted to a spot a few hundred yards west of us, by a great number of buzzards ; some on the ground, and others sitting on the trees, or flying around in the air. Approaching the place, we

saw a light, bateau-fashioned canoe, split and
shattered, lying on the top of the bank, just in the
edge of the woods ; and looking about a few minutes, found not far from the canoe, a man in a
high state of putrefaction, who had been drowned
probably a week before, in attempting to cross
from Point Au Plait to the bay.　His face and
neck were entirely destroyed by the buzzards ;
but from his dress, a drab-coloured capot, over-
alls, and moccasons, and his skin, seen by opening his calico shirt, it was evident that he was a
Canadian Frenchman.

　The cause of our detention, and of our having
been repeatedly driven back by storms, was immediately explained by Tom ; who declaring that
the Almighty would not suffer us to cross the
lake while this man lay unburied, instantly seized
the poor Frenchman's paddle, which lay near
him, and, with the aid of another sailor, working
sometimes with his hands, and sometimes with a
stick, in about an hour succeeded in digging, in
the soft sandy ground on the top of the bank, a
grave about two feet deep, into which the corpse,
dragged up by the shoulders, being placed, Tom
drew from his pocket a prayer book, and opening it at the burial service, handed it to the captain, who read it with great solemnity.　The
grave was now filled up, the paddle, with its
blade upward, was planted at its head, and over
it were thrown brush and logs, for its protection ; when, satisfied that we had done a good
work, we returned to our boat, and on board the
sloop ; where Tom, having in about an hour

prepared us an excellent dinner of fish and potatoes, we ate with great *gout ;* our appetites, from the exercise of the morning, being very keen. The wind still continued to blow strongly from the east, and the lake outside of the bay was very rough ; but on Wednesday, the 13th of April, the one changing to the southeast, and the other becoming calm, we again set sail, and on Friday evening anchored safely opposite to Fort Erie. On the following morning, taking leave of the sloop's crew, I went on shore with the captain, who introduced me to the officer commanding the fort, at the same time delivering him a letter written by Col. England. I was detained here only a few hours, when, being placed on board a small barge, in charge of a corporal and four soldiers, I was in a few hours conveyed to Fort Chippewa, a block house, garrisoned by a lieutenant and thirty men, on the north side of Chippewa creek, a few rods from its mouth, and about two miles above the falls of Niagara. Here passing the night, on the following morning, accompanied by a man whom the lieutenant had provided to conduct me, I walked down to the falls, and after spending about two hours in veiwing that stupendous cataract, proceeded to Queenstown, where, finding a wood boat going down to Fort Niagara, I immediately got on board, and arriving there an hour after, and delivering a letter to the commanding officer, was by him conducted to the quarters of Lieutenant Hill, where I was received with great kindness.

CHAPTER XI.

Spends his time very agreeably in the family of Mr. Hill at Fort Niagara—Arrives at Canandaigua in the care of Mr. Morris—Kindness of that gentleman—Arrives at his sister's in Elizabethtown, New-Jersey.

FORTY years since, the southwestern part of the state of New-York was almost an unbroken wilderness; and excepting a log ferry house on the top of the high bank opposite Queenstown (near the present site of Lewistown) there was but one house on the road, or rather footpath, between Niagara and Canandaigua, a distance of a hundred miles, and that was a tavern near the western bank of the Genesee, probably ten miles south of the spot where Rochester now stands. The best mode of travelling then was on horseback; but as there was little communication between the western part of New-York and Niagara, opportunites such as would be suitable for my return to my friends seldom occurred. I had, therefore, to wait patiently until such opportunity should offer, or until Gov. Simcoe should provide some mode of conveyance. However, I was very comfortably situated in the family of Mr. Hill, and spent my time quite pleasantly for about a week that I remained at the fort. Lieutenant Hill was adjutant of the fiftieth regiment of infantry; a part of which, with a company of artillery, garrisoned Fort Niagara, and a part was stationed at York, U. C., on the west side of the lake, nearly opposite. Frequently, by his invitation, I accompanied him, when he marched the troops, not on duty, out of the garrison (which he did on every fair day) for the purpose of exercising them. It is astonishing to see with what precision the British regulars go through the manual exercise, march, and perform the different military evolutions, and how quickly the slightest error or fault is noticed by the officer, who not unfrequently punishes the delinquent by a stroke with his rattan, over the knuckles or on the shins. The troops here, though almost perfectly disciplined, were, I thought, inferior to the twenty-fourth; who, beside, made a much more showy, and, as I conceived, a more martial appearance. The uniform of the twenty-fourth was a white vest and pantaloons, with black half gaiters; a long scarlet coat, faced with deep green and laced with silver at the button holes, skirts, and wrists. That of the fiftieth, was drab underclothes, and long scarlet coats faced with light green, without any ornament. The former wore their long hair powdered, clubbed at the neck, and spreading like a fan between their shoulders; the latter had their hair cued. With Mr. Hill I was much pleased. He appeared to be what is generally termed a clever man; plain, yet urbane in his manners—not brilliant. His principal recommendation was his natural kindness and frankness, his sociability as a companion, and his punctual observance of his duty as an officer. Being at least fifteen years younger than his wife, whom he treated rather with deference than with affection, I think it probable, that fortune, rank, or some consideration other than love, influenced his union with her. His wife was at least forty; tall and lean, with large and homely features; in her dress, very neat and simple; polished, though rather precise in her manners; quite intelligent and fluent, and possessing a very amiable disposition. During my stay with her, she treated me with the kindness of a mother, carefully repairing my shirts and clothes; and when I left her, presenting me with a calico needle and thread case, that I might learn to mend my own clothes, when occasion should require. This I carefully preserved for many years, often finding it useful; and from the habit formed when young, have ever since carried a needle and thread in my pocket book; and often thus have been led gratefully to remember that benevolent lady. The situation of Fort Niagara was a very commanding one; standing on the high bank at the mouth of the strait connecting lakes Erie and Ontario; and the scenery around it was at once romantic, grand, and sublime. Above, were the high precipitous banks, or rather mountains covered to the water's edge with trees and huge masses of rock, between which the broad and mighty water, contracted below the deafening cataract into a comparatively narrow stream, boiling and foaming, and whirling along the mighty chasm, rushed for several miles with resistless impetuosity. A few miles below, on the Canadian side, seemingly hanging on the face of the mountainous bank, stood the large white mess house, and

quarters of the Queen's rangers, constituting the
principal buildings of Queenstown, and on a
small plain between the termination of this hill
and the lake shore, was the small, but neat village
of Newark, then the residence of Gov. Simcoe.
On the west, and north, and east, the dark, deep
waters of Ontario, presented a vast expanse,
bounded only by the horizon, and inspired the
beholder with mingled wonder, delight, and awe.
Here, especially in the " still night," you might
hear the deep, heavy roar of the mighty cataract,
as the coming of the desolating tornado; and,
indeed, it may be heard distinctly, " as the sound
of many waters," on Lake Erie, more than twenty
miles distant.   I shall never forget the sensations
with which I first heard it ; sensations growing
more and more intense, as I approached nearer
and nearer to it ; nor the feeling of apprehension,
with which, while passing down the rapid current
of the river, I bent my body instinctively to the
shore as if to make the boat cling to it. Glancing
the eye from the first small break of the water
(close to the British shore, just above the head
of the long narrow island, extending almost from
the mouth of Chippewa to the falls, and at the
foot of which, formerly there was a small mill)
in the direction of Goat Island, to the middle of
the river, you are struck with dread as you mark
the second break, (as it is called,) where a
part of the mighty river, sweeping down a steep
ledge of rock, rises and rolls, in fearful swells,
that threaten instant destruction. But no language can describe the feelings of the beholder

when standing just in front of the awful precipice, he first sees the vast volume of water, rushing over, far beyond the angular summit rock, (its upper bed,) extending from its western bank to Goat Island, and plunging down, down into the deep abyss; then measures with his eye the giddy height of the foot of that island, rising pependicular from the depths below, and presenting a face of solid rock; then views the beautiful unbroken sheet of water, that falls between it and the eastern bank, facing the west, and in front of which, in clear, warm sunshine, may be always seen a brilliant rainbow, with its ample arch spanning its width; then the troubled water, rising and bounding from its fearful plunge, back to the foot of the tremendous cataract, there forced again into the dread abyss, again emerging, rolls tumultuously down, a mighty torrent. But I had not intended to have attempted even this faint outline of this most grand, sublime, and wonderful of nature's works, to describe which would require the pen of a Milton; and in beholding which the mind is led involuntarily to exclaim, "Great and marvellous are thy works, Lord God, almighty!"

I had been about a week at Fort Niagara, when one afternoon Mr. Hill informed me that an opportunity offering for me to return to my friends, Gov. Simcoe had directed that I should immediately be sent over to Newark. Tying up my small wardrobe in my handkerchief, in a few minutes I was ready to comply with this brief notice; then taking a hasty leave of Mr. and

Mrs. Hill, I was soon conveyed across the Niagara, and conducted to the house of Gov. Simcoe. The governor received me with great courtesy, and introducing me to Thomas Morris, Esq., of Canandaigua, who had arrived at Newark only the day before, remarked, that he had acquainted that gentleman with the request that had been made to him by the British minister (at the instance of my friends) to ascertain where I was, and to release me from captivity, and of the fortunate result of his efforts; and concluded by saying, that Mr. Morris, on his request, had kindly consented to take me as far as Canandaigua. Mr. Morris then made some inquiries about my family and relatives; said he was well acquainted with my uncle, Col. Ogden of Elizabethtown, N. J.; that he would with pleasure convey me to Canandaigua, whence, he had no doubt, I would have an opportunity of returning to my friends. In answering the inquiries made of me by Gov. Simcoe, I was led to speak of the conduct of Col. Elliot; particularly of his leaving me in charge of the Indians, at the mouth of the Maumee, and of the injury I had suffered, and of the danger I had in consequence incurred. On hearing this, he appeared to be quite indignant; he spoke of his instructions to Elliot to convey me to Detroit; and I well recollect his remark to Mr. Morris, that such conduct in a British officer would have subjected him to trial before a court martial; but that he was obliged to overlook many improprieties in the agents who had such influence with the

Indians, and were so necessary to his majesty in his intercourse with them. Mr. Morris, now remarking that he proposed to set off from the ferry house early next morning, and that he would wait for me until evening at Queenstown, arose and took his leave. Of Gov. Simcoe's person, I have not a distinct recollection. I remember, however, that his figure was commanding, his features were manly, his countenance was open, his manners, though dignified, were affable ; and in his conversation he had all the frankness of the soldier. I had the honour of taking tea that afternoon with his lady, a very handsome and intelligent woman, but unfortunately afflicted with so great an impediment in her speech, that, to me, it was painful to converse with her. After tea a servant appeared at the gate with two fine bay horses ; on one of which, after taking leave of Governor Simcoe and his lady, I mounted, when the servant receiving his orders, " Spin him along," we set off at a rapid canter, and travelling at half speed, up hill and down, in less than an hour arrived at Queenstown. Crossing the Niagara about dusk, and ascending the high bank, Mr. Morris and I entered the ferry house where we found Mr. Nathaniel Gorham, (if I mistake not, one of the proprietors of Canandaigua,) and a coloured servant, who had travelled with him to the frontier. Here we spent the night, and on the next morning, after a very early breakfast, set out on horseback (a separate horse being provided for me) for Canandaigua. Travelling rapidly,

and stopping only an hour at noon, to bait our
horses and take a luncheon of biscuit and
cheese, we rested at night at an Indian village;
and on the next day dining at about twelve
o'clock, at a tavern near the west bank of the
Genesee, arrived at Canandaigua a little after
dark; thus performing a journey of nearly a
hundred miles, through the wilderness, along a
footpath, in two days. Here I was placed in the
family of Mr. Sandford, a tavernkeeper, with
whom Mr. Morris (being then single, and not
having quite finished his large and elegant house
at the west end of the town) boarded. Canandaigua was, in 1793, a neat village, containing, I
think, about forty houses, scattered along the
principal street, leading westwardly from the
long narrow lake after which it was named, for
more than a mile. At the head of this street,
facing the lake, stood the house of Mr. Sandford,
a large two-story wooden building, painted white,
and making a very respectable appearance.—
Near this house, on the north, was the village
school house, where Mr. Upham taught about
forty girls and boys; and below it, was the
residence of Mr. Chapin, agent for the Senecas,
the eldest of whose sons traded with the Indians,
exchanging his goods for furs and skins; while
a younger one acted as an interpreter. At Canandaigua I remained until about the middle of
June, waiting for an opportunity to go to New-
York; at which time Mr. Chapin, having collected a large quantity of furs, and bear and
deer skins sufficient to load a pretty large bateau,

being ready to set out for New-York to replenish his stock of goods, at the request of Mr. Morris, consented to take me with him. I had spent my time very pleasantly at Canandaigua, where I had employed a part of my time at school, with Mr. Upham, and occasionally had amused myself in fishing, at the outlet of the lake. I had been treated, too, by Mr. and Mrs. Sandford, with parental kindness ; but never from a stranger did I receive such benevolent and generous treatment as I received from Mr. Morris. He had incurred the expense of purchasing a horse to convey me from Niagara ; he had defrayed the charge of my boarding and schooling at Canandaigua ; he had furnished me with some summer clothing, and now that I was ready to set out for New-York, supplied me with money to bear my expenses ; and for all this he would never afterward receive the least remuneration.

I was deeply affected when I took my leave of him, and to this day when I think of him, it is with feelings of the liveliest gratitude. Our bateau lay in the outlet, about three miles north of the north end of Canandaigua lake, to which point there was water sufficient for bateau navigation. From this point, having loaded the bateau with peltries, conveyed in wagons from the village, we proceeded slowly down the narrow winding outlet ; sometimes being obliged to stop and cut away trees that had fallen across it, and sometimes to get out and drag our flat-bottomed boat over the ripples. In this way we proceeded for nearly four days ; passing, however, the several outlets of the Seneca and Cayuga, the Owasco and other lakes, the stream gradually became larger, and its obstructions fewer. On the fourth day we arrived at the mouth of the Oneida outlet, here called Three River Points, distant from Canandaigua, by land, about sixty miles, but at least one hundred by water. Ascending the outlet, we crossed the Oneida lake, about thirty miles in length, to the mouth of Wood creek, up which small, crooked stream, we with much difficulty forced our bateau, to within a mile of the Mohawk, whence, transporting it across the ground where Rome now stands, but where then, on the Mohawk, stood but a solitary house, we proceeded down that river to Schenectady. From this place, (Mr. Chapin conveying his peltries in wagons,) we rode to Albany; whence, having stayed a day or two, we embarked on board a Dutch sloop, for New-York, where we arrived on the second day of July. Here I took leave of Mr. Chapin, and on the next day, taking a passage in an open ferry boat, (the only ferry boats in use at that time,) across the bay, in which, by a sudden gust of wind, we were nearly upset, I arrived at Elizabethtown, New-Jersey, where my sister and relations were delighted to see me. But the happiness I experienced in returning to the home of my childhood, after an absence of nearly three years, in which I had endured so many privations and hardships, and encountered so many dangers, must have been far superior to theirs; and when on the evening of that day I retired to rest, gratefully

reflecting on the past goodness and mercy of God to me, devoutly, on my knees, I thanked him for the exercise of his gracious providence toward me, preserving, sustaining, and protecting me, and restoring me in safety to my friends. The next day, being the fourth of July, there was a very splendid celebration at Elizabethtown, which I enjoyed very much. At this time, I had the pleasure of seeing my distant relative, the late Governor Bloomfield, who was highly gratified with the narrative of my captivity, and my account of Indian manners and customs; and took great pleasure in hearing my Indian songs, and in seeing me dance after the Indian mode. On the next day he caused to be published, in Kollock's "New-Jersey Journal," in substance, the following notice : "Arrived at this place, on the third inst., by the way of Detroit, Niagara, and New-York, the only son of Col. Oliver Spencer, late a captive among the Indians, with whom he remained about eight months, acquiring a considerable knowledge of their language, customs, and manners." I think, too, that there was some allusion to my looks and manners, as slightly resembling the Indians.

This notice brought people from far and near to see me; some, no doubt, merely from the regard they bore to an old and esteemed friend or acquaintance, whose son I was; but the greater part from mere curiosity, as they would flock to an exhibition of wild beasts, expecting, no doubt, to see something at least half savage. At first, I took pleasure in giving an account of my captivity; in answering the numerous inquiries that were made of me, and in singing and dancing Indian, and uttering the various Indian yells; performing so naturally, as they supposed, and exhibiting, as they fancied, such a wildness in my looks and manners, that some frequently remarked in an under tone, "How much he looks like an Indian!" but being obliged to repeat the same story, and answer the same questions, frequently twenty times a day, to different companies and individuals, I became so heartily tired of it, that at last, I gave only brief answers, often uttering a simple yes, or no, to the inquiries that were made of me. Indeed from the circumstance

of my then repeating so often the story of my
captivity, and for weeks answering so many inquiries, I became averse to say any thing about
it, and acquired a habit of replying so laconically
to questions asked me, that in after life, I have
felt mortified, when, by my brief answers to questions on this subject, I have seemed to check
farther inquiry, and to give room to suspect me
of a want of politeness, or even of civility.

My long narrative, which must have exercised
the patience of the reader, may soon be brought
to a close.   At Elizabethtown, I remained with
my sister and brother-in-law Mr. Halstead, for
a little more than two years ; a regular portion
of all of which time was occupied by me at
school ; and on the 14th of September, 1795,
being then fourteen years old, I set out on horseback, in company with a Mr. Crane, and the late
General Schenck, (then on his first visit to the
west,) on my return home.   We performed the
journey to Pittsburg in ten days, and there
putting our horses on board a flat boat, descended
the Ohio, and arrived at Columbia about the
middle of October.   The joy of my parents, on
seeing me, is more easily imagined than described ; with tears and embraces, they welcomed my return.   The day was spent in affectionate inquiries about the past ; and devoutly,
and gratefully that evening, around our family
altar, did we join in thanksgiving and praise,
with my pious father, to the Father of mercies,
for all his past unmerited goodness ; particu-

larly, for my preservation, and safe restoration
to my home.

Nearly forty years have since passed away;
our rivers teem with commerce; their banks are
covered with farms, with houses, villages, towns,
and cities; the wilderness has been converted
into fruitful fields; temples to God are erected,
where once stood the Indian wigwam, and the
praises of the Most High resound, where formerly the screams of the panther, or the yell of the
savage only were heard. O, "What hath God
wrought?" But where are the friends and companions of our youth? Our parents, where are
they? Mine have long since "slept with their
fathers." Wawpawwawquaw, who only a short
time since, had for several years previously paid
me an annual visit, has gone to the land of his
fathers and almost all of those of whom in my
narrative I have spoken, are no longer "dwellers
upon earth." We, also, will soon end our
earthly pilgrimage, and enter into "that bourne
whence no traveller returns." May we through
Divine grace "finish well our journey," that we
may dwell at last, where "ever-during spring
abides, and never-withering flowers;" in that
healthful clime, where "sickness, sorrow, pain,
and death, are felt and feared no more;" where
"there is fulness of joy," and where there are
"pleasures for evermore."

CONTENTS.

CHAPTER I.

CHAPTER II.

CHAPTER III.

CHAPTER IV.

CHAPTER V.

CHAPTER VI.

CHAPTER VII.

CHAPTER VIII.

CHAPTER IX.

CHAPTER X.

CHAPTER XI.